STOP WAITING FOR PERMISSION!

Why We Take No for an Answer and What You Can Do About It

by Steve Truitt

Havenhurst Books
Los Angeles

Havenhurst Books, Los Angeles 90046
© 2009 by Havenhurst Books
All rights reserved. Published 2009
Printed in the United States of America
14 13 12 11 10 09 5 4 3 2 1
ISBN 978-0-9822853-1-2 0-9822853-1-0
Truitt, Steve
Stop Waiting for Permission! Why We Take No
for an Answer and What You Can Do About It

Book Cover Concept: Harleen Mittal
Book Cover Design: Paul Stephenson
Interior Design: Jeny Lyn B. Ruelo and Ralph Rhodden Cavero

CONTENTS

For my wife and two daughters:
I love every day.

And for my grandfather:
Thank you for the inspiration to find
greatness in the most unlikely of places.
Rest in magnificent peace and legacy.

FOREWORD
WHAT IS YOUR PROMISE TO YOURSELF?

I can't tell you how many times I have tried to jump-start my life! You know, transform, re-invent, re-create. The idea of a life "do-over" is so alluring because it always lingers out there in the realm of what's possible. It's also more than a little daunting. Sometimes we promise ourselves this time will be different, but we end up right back at the starting position.

If you're like me, you know in your head that most things in life are sweetened by risk, but taking risks – especially in times like these – is not too appetizing. As a businesswoman, celebrity (whatever THAT means) , and mother of three, I know firsthand how a lack of energy and destructive habits can affect you and all the lives you touch every day. Easy to see; hard to change. That's why I'm so glad I've had the chance to meet and share inspiration with Steve Truitt, and I know after reading this book, you'll feel the same way.

When I first met Steve, it was at the dedication of my star on the Hollywood Walk of Fame. He was a brand new reporter and told me that I was his very first interview. I must not have been too hard on him, because he kept at it! Ten years later we reconnected at the California Governor & First Lady's Conference on Women where he was collecting interviews for this book, and I was thrilled to see his evolution and hear about his emergence as a hypnotherapist, life coach, and TV & Radio personality! Since then we have had countless conversations about his philosophy of not taking "No" for an answer, his love for sharing personal empowerment, and his passion for this book. We are both "self-help" junkies who are likely never to find a 12-step cure. I thought I had heard it all when Steve shared his message: "Know yourself, don't NO yourself." I understood that instantly. We close ourselves off from so many things that would be life-enhancing , soul-stretching experiences by saying NO! It's only when we dare to venture outside our comfort zone that we truly grow, and Steve's mantra has a resonance that can be felt by anyone struggling to get beyond his or her own mental roadblocks and know themselves.

When I got the offer to appear on season 4 of *Dancing with the Stars* I was excited, yet completely frightened and insanely worried! Would I be able to last? Would I be able to learn those routines? Would my kids be supportive? How would fit into those outfits? How would I manage to run my company and non-profit foundation and still have time to do the fox trot and the mambo? Well first thing I did was call a life coach who sat me down and opened my eyes to realize where all this fear was coming from. The question I had always been asking myself was "Will I be enough?" She helped me realize that yes, indeed "I am enough." It's not whether I win or lose, fail or succeed; it's all about being safe and secure in knowing that whatever the outcome, I will always be enough, regardless of having danced the world's worst *paso doble* in front of 25 million people!

After that experience I created Sheer Inspiration Coaching to bring the revitalizing, transformational power of a personal life coach to women. It's not just about motivation and positive thinking. It's about a customized plan for your life developed with a real expert who understands your unique needs and circumstances. The right coach can spend as little as a few minutes with someone and begin a revolution of change, and this is the ability Steve Truitt possesses with grace and dexterity, humor and insight.

In *Stop Waiting For Permission!* you'll discover Steve's proven method for changing your life and getting rid of the "No's" that get in your way. You'll learn what "The Three P's of Prosperity" are, and how they can magically transform your life. You'll read interviews with Arnold Schwarzenegger, Jenny McCarthy, Maria Shriver, Burt Rutan, Suze Orman, and so many more about their winning philosophies in life! He'll challenge you with homework at the end of each chapter designed to shake loose your old ways, and point you in the direction of your dreams!

Do you feel like you could be happier? Are you searching for a stronger balance within your life? Are you prepared to step into your power, claim the life you know is waiting for you, and re-create yourself? Then *Stop Waiting For Permission* is the perfect book for you right now.

We all want to be heard. We all want to know that we're not alone. We all dream about changing, and accomplishing our goals. Remember, the most important relationship you will ever have in life is the one with yourself... when you learn to know yourself and not "No" yourself, as Steve teaches, I know you're going to find peace and prosperity on a deeply personal level.

So give yourself permission to open up and enjoy.... ready, set---CHANGE!

– Leeza Gibbons

PROLOGUE
A BRIEF HISTORY OF THE HUMAN SPIRIT

Sixty-five million years ago an asteroid roughly six miles across slammed into the Yucatan Peninsula in a place now known as Chicxulub, Mexico. The cataclysmic impact and resulting effects on the environment is believed to be the reason for the extinction of the dinosaurs. Without that event, dinosaurs might today still be roaming the earth as the dominant species, and man – if he were to have developed at all – would be hiding in holes and caves searching for food whenever or wherever he could find it, if indeed he wasn't food for someone else!

But that didn't happen. Smaller mammals, including man, rose from the ashes over millions of years and the dinosaurs that once ruled the planet became simply and ironically... oil.

Sixty-five million years later, in January 2009, a US Airways flight made an emergency ditching shortly after take-off from New York's LaGuardia airport. An unusual double engine bird strike, which shut down both engines, forced the pilot to bring his plane down in the icy waters of the Hudson River. All aboard survived the crash for two very specific reasons: One, the pilot and the crew were trained for such an emergency; and two, the passengers, while terrified, were careful, determined and calm. In a *Time* Magazine article the next week, Amanda Ripley, author of *The Unthinkable: Who Survives When Disaster Strikes – And Why*, wrote "Imagine if this had been a scene from *24*, if terrorists – not geese – had taken out the engines. The heroes would have been the rescuers – Special Forces soldiers dangling from helicopters, Jack Bauer speed boating down the Hudson – and the passengers would have been shrieking, panicking, useless. The truth is... regular people are quite capable of wrestling open exit doors. Ferry captains, without waiting for orders, will make a beeline for trouble. We have the power to save ourselves. And we are more resilient than we think."

Consider the idiom that military leaders, athletes, and law enforcement professionals live by: "When challenged or in a crisis, you don't rise to the level of the situation, you sink to the level of your training!"

I believe that, in our evolution, we humans are just getting started. What will allow us to thrive in any situation will ultimately be our training, the training we give ourselves every day. This book was written to be a part of that training.

INTRODUCTION

THE BALLAD OF MEL CHANG

Mel Chang was a forty-four-year-old employee of Federal Express. He had been with the company for twenty-three years, starting as a deliveryman, eventually working his way up to mid-level manager. He lived in Redondo Beach, California. During the week he devoted most of his time to the job, often rising at 4:30 in the morning and not coming home until 7:00 in the evenings. On the weekends, to relieve stress, Mel rode his race bike around and through the South Bay, often biking for more than thirty or forty miles at a time.

His friends and family loved him, his co-workers respected him, and his company valued him. Mel was my neighbor, and a great one. My wife and I rarely saw Mel, as he was always working at the office, but when we did, he always had a smile for us. On the weekends when I needed a hand, or a tool from his garage, he was always happy to lend whatever he could. He bought our daughter a very nice blanket on the occasion of her birth, and he made sure to keep me updated on anything I needed to know about my home's upkeep. (We lived next door to each other in nearly identical houses).

I found Mel dead in his kitchen on a Monday evening, two weeks before Christmas, 2005. He had been dead for two days. While no official cause of death was released to friends, it was clear to all of us that Mel died of a stress-related heart attack. His job – as he said to me frequently – was literally killing him.

Mel gave his life for his job, and he died way too young. What's worse is that he never chose to leave the company... a choice that he knew was doing him harm.

"That's the way it is," he would tell me about his stressful career, "what are you gonna do?"

What I decided to do was write this book, and in the process, honor the memory and legacy of Mel Chang, and all those who have either inspired me, or sought inspiration from me and others like me who have found great joy, satisfaction, and purpose in being of service to others.

THE THREE P'S OF PROSPERITY

Around the time of Mel's death, I was still considering taking on life-coaching full time. I had become increasingly fascinated with the science of Neuro-Linguistic Programming (NLP), a discipline I had become certified in several years earlier. NLP is an interpersonal communication model and an alternative approach to psychotherapy based on the subjective study of language, communication and how they affect personal change, with the aim of discovering successful patterns of behavior. NLP practitioners work with the unconscious minds of clients to rebuild and restructure language, which serves the client's goals for success, prosperity, happiness, and self worth. Simply put, we help train your brain to be good to you!

I began to have increased success with the people I was coaching, and realized that there was a direct link between the traumatic discovery of finding my dead friend in his kitchen and the results I was getting with my clients, a sense of "This is the only time we have. Now. Let's make something of it!" I began to see a pattern not only in our own past behaviors, but also in what I consider to be an epidemic: Many of us are waiting for someone or something to define us; tell us who we are; validate our choices; or give our existence meaning.

We're waiting for permission to have the life we dream of having.

And that word, *waiting*, was the spark for me. I began to coach my clients – and myself – under the strict doctrine that we are never allowed to complain about that which we simply allow to happen. So many of us dwell in our situations, never willing to change them, but are fully capable of spending all our energy grousing about them over and over to whomever will listen to the point where our complaints become our identity.

This understanding became the impetus for *The THREE P's Of Prosperity: Purpose; Permission; Position.* All three aspects of the system rely on the others to work and rely on the order of their sequence to be effective.

This book evolved with that system in mind. I was no longer willing to just be an observer of the phenomenon, but instead decided to take action and do something about it. I woke up one morning and said to myself, "I should write a book." Then the very next thing that I said was, "Everybody says that, Steve. Everyone says they should write a book about an idea or concept or story they have, but they rarely do. Is that you? Are you going to be that guy who says he should write a book and then doesn't?" The challenge was too hard to ignore. I began a nearly three-year journey that would take me on the most incredible, soul-searching and patience-testing ride of my life. My goal was to write a motivational book that would inspire millions of people to stop taking "No" for an answer – *especially from themselves* – and take on a newer, more powerful way of being, based on the Three P's of Prosperity.

Stop Waiting For Permission! is for you. My intention is to help you find within yourself that hidden "switch" that when flicked on will light up for you all the possibility you've always had, but have never known was there. Or perhaps you've been waiting on someone or something else to give you the permission to achieve your goals. There has never been a better time for this book to come to you. If you've lived your life knowing that something is missing for you... fearing financial crisis because you've always waited for a paycheck, or worked for someone else... wondering if what you have is all you'll ever have... fearing change or growth... angry or sad over lost opportunities or past mistakes... or just stagnated by your own apathy toward life in general, this book has found you for a reason. Enjoy and be inspired by the stories and the interviews, DO THE HOMEWORK after each chapter, and you'll find that place inside you that you've been saying "No" to. Sometimes all it takes is a necessary, often difficult push – the permission you give yourself to have the life you were meant to live. And the timing is right... it's always right when you're ready to make a change.

Right now in these perilous times in our nation's history we are stuck. This is our Chicxulub asteroid. A major catastrophe has struck our financial system. The dominant species, stuck in antiquated thoughts and procedures, has fallen, making way for newer, smaller and necessary species to develop and take us into a new – and largely digital – age of discovery, happiness, and prosperity. In the Chinese written language, the symbol for disaster is also the symbol for opportunity.

Are you one of those people? Will you evolve from the ashes and stake your claim in the new world in which you were born to succeed? Keep reading...and maybe you will be.

Are you eager to discover the power in you that you knew was there, but didn't know how to access? Keep reading....

Or are you between loves in your life, eager to finally break the cycle of relationship failure that seems to keep following you? Keep reading.

Throughout this book you will read about clients who have come to see me to uncover the stories they told, the reasons they keep telling them, and how we worked together to let those stories go and create new possibilities. I also profile, and in most cases interview, some extraordinary people – some very famous, like Jenny McCarthy, Playmate/host-turned-activist-mother whose challenges with dealing with a special needs son brought her to the forefront of autism awareness and a possible cure. She shares with me the evolution her life has undergone and the comfort with the person she has become as a result of her challenges. I talk with financial guru Suze Orman, whose rise to fame was born from the persistence she forged in her tumultuous male-dominated beginnings at Merrill Lynch.

Iconic musician Frank Zappa's widow, Gail, sat down with me to talk about her husband – arguably one of the greatest pioneers of free speech since the constitutional framers – and his dedication to register young, civic-minded voters all around the country.

Some of my subjects are people you've heard about, but you might not recognize their names or faces: Aron Ralston, the hiker who was forced to cut his own arm off after he was trapped for six days in a cave while hiking alone; Burt Rutan, aviation pioneer who designed and built the first private space vehicle, "Space Ship One," capturing the Ansari X-Prize and the imagination of the world; Kathy Buckley, who battled total hearing loss, being run over by a jeep on the beach and a misdiagnosis of mental retardation at age three to become one of America's foremost comediennes and motivational speakers; and Patrick Reynolds, estranged heir to the R. J. Reynolds tobacco empire who turned his back on a massive family fortune and risked alienation to blow the whistle on the industry and expose the dangers of cigarette smoking.

Then there is the non-famous person, my grandfather Cecil T. Young, whose story of determination, courage, and forthrightness in a time when racial segregation was the order of the day fills me to this day with inspiration, hope, and pride. Eleven people total, all of whom lived their lives with extraordinary passion where taking "No" for an answer simply wasn't an option, will, I hope, inspire you as well.

This relentless pursuit of interviews with people who have touched my life – and no doubt yours –included the almost impossible goal of interviewing the then governor of California, Arnold Schwarzenegger. This was before the scandal broke about his affair and child out of wed lock which ultimately led to the demise of his marriage to Maria Shriver. But despite what you may think of him, to me, at the time, Mr. Schwarzenegger represented the ultimate modern example of not taking "No" for an answer. When he was a young man in Austria, he would tell his friends that he was going to move to the United States, become a huge star, and marry a Kennedy. His friends would just laugh and dismiss him. When he got to the States, the notion of him being a star was ludicrous. He was told he looked funny, no one could understand what he was saying, and his name was too long and unpronounceable. None of that stopped him. Ever. Fueled by my own resolve, I became determined early on in the process of writing this book to include an interview with Schwarzenegger about his philosophy of not taking "No" for an answer, how he learned it, and how he sustained that philosophy throughout his storied and powerful life. It wasn't always easy for me to write this book, especially taking on the task of interviewing Mr. Schwarzenegger. I was confronted with countless "No's" – even from myself where at the most crucial point when I was just a few feet away from my ultimate goal: an interview with Arnold! For nearly three years I made every effort to interview the Governor through just about every channel I could think of, and in the final hour, when I came within mere feet of my ultimate goal, and was denied for the final time the opportunity to have access, inspiration from the most unlikely of places propelled me to keep trying! You'll read more about that adventure later in the book.

For now, sit back, open your mind and heart, and get ready to create for yourself the life you deserve now. And more importantly, get ready to have it last.

PART ONE: PURPOSE

YOUR STORY

Someone once told me that early on in life, if a truck hits you, you either become the truck, or you become the victim of the truck. I have seen evidence of that in the people I have met and dealt with ever since.

At some point in your early life, something happened – outside of your realm of understanding – that forced you to make a decision about yourself based on the experience.

Here are some examples:

"My mom hit me when I was five and so I decided that I was not worthy of her love. Ever since, I've struggled with insecurity."

"My teacher told me I should have known better when I mixed the wrong color paints in my finger painting class in second grade, so I decided that from that point on I would always know better. I've been super hard on myself since then and never give myself a break."

"I heard my mother and father fighting in the next room and it was about me! I decided that their fighting was my fault, and I needed to fix it, and every other fight I encountered from then on."

"My brother beat me up as a kid, so I beat everyone else up now."

"I was put in a foster home when I was three years old

until I was five years old. I never understood why my parents abandoned me. And so now emotionally I never let anyone in. Ever."

Any of these strike a chord? If not, you may have your own story that fits this scenario.

"Everyone has their reasons," Orson Welles once explained in an interview. He was talking about how he created such rich, in-depth characters in his films and what he saw as the necessary understanding of the human condition. What Orson Welles may or may not have known is that the NLP practice that so many of us do with clients works on that exact principle: your reasons. Your story.

You may be painfully aware of your story, or it may be a complete mystery to you. But whatever the case, each of us tells the story of our life through words and deeds every single day of our existence. And I believe fully that the story we tell is rarely in sync with what our true purpose is in life. This story was created early on, crafted, honed, and perfected through time. Tested, enhanced and refined through experiences unconsciously designed by you to support the tale, it's a story whose origins take root early on in your life where the understanding of the experiences you had were clearly disconnected from the reality of the situation.

For the sake of this book, I assume that if you're reading these words, you've come to realize that perhaps the story you've been telling and living no longer serves the person you truly wish to be now. You recognize that your goals have not served your true gifts, your true talents, your true purpose, and *you're ready for a change.*

You have been a "No" to yourself and your possibility, or you've continually taken no for an answer from others. And you've done it to support a story--a story you've told to keep you from your greatest good, your greatest possibility, your greatest story: the story of you without the story.

CHAPTER ONE
THE FINISH LINE

CREATION, A STORY

Creation had been around forever. One day, Creation was bored and lonely. And so creation decided to create a partner to end the loneliness. Once the partner appeared, Creation was no longer lonely, and that lasted for a few millennia. But then Creation and the partner got bored, so they decided to create a game to play and they called it "Over there": they would point to over there and then go there. Then they would point to "over there" and go there. And that was fun and the fun lasted a few millennia, until Creation and its partner got bored again. Then they decided to add a little spice to the game by making what was "over there" better than what was over here, so going "over there" became more satisfying but still a meaningless departure. And that was fun! And that lasted a few millennia, until it got boring again. So Creation and the partner decided that in order to make sure the game never got boring again they would forget that it was just a game. They would forget that what was "over there" was no more or less important than what was "over here," and it would never be boring again. And so they did. They *forgot* it was just a meaningless game.

And that is where we are today...

WAITING

Imagine you are an Olympic-class runner, on your mark, set at the starting line. At the end of the sprint, something you've waited for your whole life: The gold metal. What is the first and only thing that has to happen – out of your control – for you to achieve that goal?

The starting gun needs to be fired.

And so there you stay, at the starting line, crouched and ready, wanting so desperately to cross the line first and bring home the gold.

But the gun never goes off. Why?

It's no secret that most of us in this culture want so desperately the things that seem out of reach, down the road, on the other side of the fence or a few months away... "Over there." Our focus for happiness seems to be narrowing on the things we don't have as if the magic pill to take which will give us happiness is just a heartbeat away, if only we had ...(fill in the blank).

But what seems to occur in our quest for "over there" is that "over there" is either never within our reach, or if it is, it ceases to be important or integral to our happiness once we get there. And we've forgotten that it's just a game.

And so for this chapter, and indeed this first section of the book, I want to focus on the endgame. The finish line. The prize. And the reasons we're so desperate to get there. I want to look at how we become so blind to our true gifts and destiny as we reach out in the dark for that which seems just within reach, but is not. But in order to do that, first I want to look at *how* and *why* we choose that which we desire.

Below is an example of a client I worked with in the fall of 2005. Her story of how she became the truck in her own life is obvious. See if you see yourself or anyone you know within this example.

MELISSA

Melissa struggled in her early life with an unavailable and regularly judgmental father. His relentless obsession with physical perfection trickled down through the family like a poison, intimidating wife, daughter, and son alike.

In Melissa's case, the result for her was an obsession with the unhealthy pursuit of physical beauty and an unconscious aversion to thoughts of marriage or children.

She moved to Los Angeles after college to pursue an acting career, along the way having major surgical alterations to her nose, breasts, lips, and hips. She got an agent and began acting classes in one of the best schools in town. She bought the latest and most expensive clothes, styled her hair with one of the best stylists in Beverly Hills, and regularly judged those around her who didn't possess the same adherence to the fashion and style fads of the moment. Her commitment to her craft was intense, and her refusal to divert from her plans of being a star was unwavering.

The result was that this woman – a complete and intensely

trained actor with a voracious hunger for stardom – managed to secure only small roles in student films where she mostly ran around in a bikini or her underwear in slow motion.

The casting associates and producers she encountered only saw one thing: her body. And despite her desire to achieve a more respectable status, she accepted her role as a shell.

But that's not the end of the story.

Melissa was – since high school – a classically-trained dancer. Her ballet training throughout high school and college led to dance performances with her troupe in locations all across the globe. Her poise was perfect, her body limber, and her presence on stage amazing.

Although she continued to keep her dancing talent in tact throughout her pursuit of an acting career, she missed out on an amazing opportunity to excel as a ballet dancer early on, choosing instead the life of an actor. By the time I met her, she was beyond the age where it was realistic to take on a career in dance, and she supported herself by teaching others privately.

Now you might say that becoming an actor was her choice, and that's her right to make it. True. But it was a choice that – by the time she came to see me – she deeply regretted.

The week she turned thirty-three years old, she attended the wedding of a close friend. Just about everyone in attendance was with someone else as a date. Melissa was a bridesmaid. She stood beside her friend and watched as she took her vows. At the reception she met the bride's aunt, a fifty-year old real estate broker from the San Fernando Valley. Being the only two single people there, they struck up a conversation. By the end of that conversation, Melissa had a profound epiphany. The older woman related her own story of staying single in order to pursue a career. Melissa told me that although the woman spoke positively about her career and life, she could see emptiness in her eyes. Whether it was real or not, Melissa felt a longing in this woman that perhaps even she did not realize was there. A light went off in Melissa's head and heart. She stood there thinking to herself "that's me in the future." That one realization was enough to shock Melissa off course enough to make a change in her life, a change that would be permanent.

When we started our work together, she identified the goal she wanted to achieve: Not only did she want to leave acting, but also she wanted to forgive herself for throwing away the opportunity of a lifetime. And something else: She wanted to fall in love, get married and have a family. Her story, finally, had changed.

THE COST OF PAST CHOICES

By the time I see my clients, they have gotten to the point in their lives where the costs of their previous harmful habits, behaviors and choices have become painfully clear. They know that what it took them to get to this point in their lives was no longer enough to make them happy like they thought it would, and they feel truly lost.

Believe it or not, that's good news. It means they're ready to see life in a different way... perhaps for the first time.

This was how I encountered Melissa. She was clear that her physical fixation and dedication to an elusive acting career had caused her to miss out on the enriching possibility of being a professional dancer and having a family.

The first thing we had to do was get her clear on the origin of her perfection-pursuit paradigm. She knew quite clearly that her father was the root cause of her looks-oriented way of life. What she didn't know was that she was responsible for buying into it.

That's the key.

She bought into her father's model of the world. She took on his perceptions. She carried on his legacy of shallowness. And worst of all, she turned her back on her true calling: Dance. And she did it all with great exuberance.

Her choice? Sure. Her responsibility? Absolutely.

But the point here is not to blame or shame. The point is that she allowed her father's prize to be her prize, and for the first time in her life she was taking responsibility for it.

Whose life are you living? Who are you succeeding for, and at what cost?

Melissa didn't need to discover that it was her father's influence that steered her choices; she needed to simply change the course of her life – a muscle she had never flexed before.

Through the course of several intense sessions, Melissa discovered that what she lacked the most – in spite of projecting extreme confidence – was the ability to trust her own instincts. Any time a thought toward a decision was brewing in her head, she ran the thought through her "father filter," so the choice then became one based on what her father's "voice" dictated. Her natural reaction to this revelation was to confront her father and tell him to shove it for screwing her up.

I had her do the opposite.

I gave her a lot of homework to do – tasks that would jar loose the framework of her old habits and begin to tear down the structure of her old paradigm. The most important project was to phone her father and query him, getting his perspective on who he was, why he thought the things he thought, and why he did the things he did. She resisted at first, fearful that no matter what she said to him it would lead to a confrontation that she would surely lose. I responded by reminding her that she was going to say nothing. Instead she would be asking him key questions – an interview if you will – to uncover his mind set. Here's a rough idea of how I had her ask:

"Dad, I'm working with a coach to make some significant and long-lasting, positive changes in my life, and because I really want you to be a part of that *new me*, I think its really important that I let go of the story I've been telling myself about you, and really get your side of the story on things. If it's alright, I'd like to ask you a few questions about things that happened in the past, in order to understand where you were coming from, since I've only had my perspective with which to look at it. Here's my first question..."

I then had her come up with several very specific examples of behavior she witnessed from her father which she felt led to her taking on her role as one fixated on physical perfection. She didn't ask him why he was that way; instead she got into his mind. One example went like this:

"Dad, when we were young, you told me that you couldn't love someone who didn't care about their appearance. I took that to mean that if I didn't take care of my appearance, then you wouldn't love ME. I would like to know if that's what you were thinking?"

And to her surprise, this was her father's response:

"I guess what I was thinking was that my father was a man who never took care of himself. He took drugs, smoked, ate way too much bad stuff, got very fat, was always sick and on top of it, was a horrible father to us and a horrible husband to my mom. He died way too early from a bad liver and diabetes, and I always hated him for it. I think what I probably meant was that I couldn't love myself if I let that happen to me."

The rest of the "interview" went on in that way. Melissa continued with observations and conclusions that she made when only a child that had no basis in reality to what was really being expressed. And although her father was admittedly a man who was driven by a healthy and attractive life style, he never wanted his daughter to feel the contempt that he felt for his father.

She didn't. She feared his judgment instead.

The result of the phone call was an opening for Melissa she never considered. For the first time in her life, she saw her father as not this impossibly distant oppressive figure, but just a man – a man who had his own life experiences – and who did the best he could with them.

Melissa got what she wanted, and more. Her relationship with her father became one of mutual respect, and her relationship with herself and her true goals transformed as well. Once she realized that her relentless pursuit of physical perfection led not to love, but isolation, she saw not just her goal, but the original reason she never attained until now.

In short, Melissa not only took on a similar obsession to what she believed her father had, but she postponed her own life out of the unconscious fear that she would pass the same problems on to her children. That's why she avoided relationships.

As of this edition, Melissa has had several other conversations with her mother, brothers, and father which have allowed her to release other stories she was supporting related to her past and to focus on the goals she truly wanted to achieve. She is in a loving and healthy marriage, and she no longer fears that she will influence her future children in the way her father influenced her.

Melissa's success is NLP in action.

KATHY BUCKLEY

It's rare to find stories as tragic and triumphant as the life of Kathy Buckley. You'll read all about her in the interview she gave me, in the meantime, here's what most Americans know about her: Billed as America's first hearing-impaired comedienne, Kathy is also a five-time American Comedy Award Nominee as Best Stand-Up Female Comedienne. As an actress, she is known for her guest starring roles on shows such as *Touched by an Angel,* and for her critically acclaimed one-woman Off-Broadway show, *Don't Buck with Me/Now Hear This!* As a motivational speaker, she inspires thousands of people around the world, sharing her story of overcoming some of the most difficult obstacles one can imagine in life, telling how she met those challenges with dignity, courage, and laughter.

Among her many honors, Kathy has received the Woman of the Year Award from the Oralingua School, American Hero Award from the City of Hope as their role model of the year, the Toastmasters International Communication and Leadership Award, the Dole Foundation Media Awareness Award for her dedication to all people with disabilities, the National Council on Communicative Disorders Individual Achievement Award, and the Hear Now Help America Hear award for her commitment to children. Kathy's first, middle, and last love is children, and her work with underprivileged kids is legendary. There's no empty wall space in her office. It's covered with not only awards and certificates, but with cards and letters from children from all over the world, thanking her for her tireless love and support for them. It doesn't take a life coach or a therapist to figure out that her own troubled beginnings were perhaps the catalyst for her work with children.

Kathy's story is not for the faint of heart.

When she was three years old, her hearing loss was

misdiagnosed as retardation and she was placed in a school for the mentally retarded. She remained there until she was eight years old, without any real grasp of language, reading or proper forms of communication. Without the ability to protect herself or understand what was going on around her, most of Kathy's first decade was tragically wasted. On top of that, her disability caused frustration with her family and peers. Often she was smacked, slapped, or kicked by a family member or schoolmate. To this day she doesn't know why, but she assumes it was because they could not reach her any other way.

Then at age eight, her hearing impairment was correctly diagnosed, so she was transferred to a school where she received the proper care and attention. Her teacher, Joan Daley, taught her how to talk by using a balloon for vibrations. Daley would blow up the balloon and talk to Kathy through it. By feeling her vibrations, Kathy could identify her own, and thus she learned the basic tenets of language. Kathy attributes her love for children to her time with Ms. Daley, noting: "When you have a hearing loss, facial expressions are crucial to a deaf child, and a lot of times when someone is trying to communicate to a deaf child, they always have this question mark on their face... and that question mark feels like a rejection to someone who's looking for communication and acceptance in facial expressions. But Ms. Joan Daley never had a question mark on her face... she always had a smile on her face and a sparkle in her eye, and she always looked me right in the eye because she knew I could read her lips, and she was very patient and caring and loving. And she did something no one else ever did for me... she spoke about herself, she would tell me stories about herself – now whether they were true or not, I don't know, but she would then have me repeat the stories to see how much of them I was getting. And as a result, I ended up being a storyteller in my comedy!"

Kathy progressed so rapidly, it was decided that she would return to public school, where Kathy says she had no business being. She stood out immediately. She had to wear a hearing-enhancement device clipped to her ears with wires running down to a battery pack on her chest. Awkward and often alone, she did what she could to fit in, eventually stealing and getting in trouble, looking for acceptance.

Kathy graduated high school, but had a 1.0 grade average. By the time she was eighteen, she had tried to commit suicide on five different occasions, all the time confused as to who she was supposed to be.

At nine years old she was molested by a person she refers to as "close to the family." When she was sixteen, she was raped by a classmate. All the time throughout her early years she could never understand why these things were happening to her. She had neither the language nor the context to make sense of it all, resorting to her own interpretation: "I'm a reject." And the worst was yet to come.

When Kathy was nineteen, lying on the beach sunbathing, she was run over by a lifeguard in a Jeep who never saw her. She never heard him coming. As the truck barreled over her, she rolled to protect her head, but in doing so she caused more damage to her rib cage and arms. The Jeep ran over her face stomach, chest, thighs and back. She was in and out of the hospital for five years and in and out of a wheel chair for two years after that. Doctors told her she would never walk again, and in true Kathy style she quips: "I figured I didn't hear them, so I just got up and left!"

I met Kathy Buckley at her home one lazy Sunday morning and was wowed immediately by her graciousness and open nature. She invited me to her home outside of Los Angeles and, from the first second I met her, she called me – a complete stranger – "sweetie." We sat for nearly an hour for our first interview, and I have since had her on my radio show. The transcript below draws from both interviews.

You clearly love working with children. What does it mean to you?

You give your child what you didn't have. And I believe that every child on this planet is my responsibility, and if everyone thought that way, there would be no harm done to a child. Every child is a gift and they should know that. At my school "No Limits" we have kids as old as five years old who can't even say their own name. Kids are the best thing on the planet and we took the time and patience to listen to them, we could learn a lot. Listen to a kid: you might just learn something.

Isn't it true that so many adults feel they have to enforce their own vision on a child instead of letting them learn?

Parent and adults talk at kids. But with my godchild, I listen to her. Who am I to tell her who she is? I want her to find it out for herself, so I listen. A lot of kids don't understand what their parents' lives were like as kids, and so they don't know how to be a kid themselves... they look at their parents as they are now – telling them what to do and be. Parents should teach children how to pick themselves up from mistakes and problems, not scolding them for them.

You seem to take every challenge and turn it into the positive. You say look for the positive... 90% of the negative that happens is created by our choices. How do you find the ability to choose powerful, forward thinking, instead of being spiteful and hating God for all that you went through?

You know, I died at the scene of that Jeep accident. And I spent the first twenty years of my life looking for three things: love, warmth, and acceptance. When I died that day, I got a love that you can't even fathom in this world... you can't even imagine it! And I got an acceptance and knowledge that I am totally unconditionally loved – flaws and all. Then I got a fourth gift that no one had ever given me to that point in my life: the gift of choice. Someone, somewhere loved me so much that they let me make the decision as to whether I was going to continue on, or give up and die.

When you spend your whole life looking for love, there's something about the gift of choice – It's not that you always get your choice, but it's the opportunity to have your brain think about yourself.   My whole life was "Why can't she can't read, why can't she can't write?" All that stuff was happening up until the accident. Then I realized that I was given a choice, and if someone loves me that much to give me that gift, then I should at least love myself somewhat. And if I make the choice to be here, then I'm going to make the most of it. For my first twenty years, my life consisted of everybody else's vocabulary. My belief system was what everyone else was saying about me, or for me, and I never got to know who Kathy was. And not just in the eyes of man, but also in the eyes of God.

And the answer, apparently, was trying stand-up. How did you stumble into that?

It was a contest. I met Geri Stewart, the first comedienne with cerebral palsy, and we were at a comedy night to raise money for the cause. And I kept pacing outside, thinking "Will I hear them call me onstage?" And people are asking me "How long have you been doing comedy?" and I kept telling everybody it was my first time ever. I mean there were comedians there who had been doing stand up anywhere from three to ten years! Then finally when I was called on stage, it was like a blanket of faith that fell on me. I went on stage in front of 250 people and started telling my stories, telling my jokes. And the laughter... I couldn't really hear them, but I could see their faces laughing and laughing. And I ended up winning the contest that night!

And what I didn't know was that if you won that contest, you had to then go to semi-finals, which means more jokes, and I ended up placing fourth among eighty experienced comedians.

You said you just told your story... how did you know that your particular balance of tragedy and comedy was going to work?

There is nothing in life that's that serious. It's that simple. You have to look at every situation that comes into your life as a momentary thing. If you take something negative and you give it life with your thoughts and fears, the more words and attention you put in to it, the more life you're going to give it, and the more miserable you're going to be. If something comes into your life that doesn't belong there, find a solution to it, or let it go. My humor comes from the stupidity of how people look at things and look for the negative. I'm all about the positive. I'm all about moving on. I realize that life is a gift given. When I was young, I wasn't living; I was just existing to be accepted into a society that didn't want me. And it's funny because hearing people see me as deaf, but deaf people see me as hearing because I can speak and hear somewhat. So I decided I would create my own world, and anybody and everybody is welcome... there will be no judgments passed upon them. I mean I've been able to forgive the person who molested me to the point that we have a beautiful relationship today. My belief system is... whatever happened 5, 15, 25 years ago, is in the past, not in the present. And people do change. If you're willing to grow, then you have to trust that other people are as well.

I am blessed enough to have had a second chance at life and I'm going to live it, but not with the vocabulary I was raised with everybody's ignorance telling me I can't, I can't, I can't.

I can do anything I want to do... except get a date, apparently. I mean my last relationship was eighteen years ago, and I'm thinking, hey, a girl needs her space!

. . .

THE PRIZE

In order to feel like a winner, Melissa stood on that track with her eye solely on the prize; the finish line. And by only needing to win, she was never actually in the race. She never ran the steps, never got up to speed, never stumbled, never built up a sweat, and never saw the value of running, sweating, or stumbling and getting back up. By living in the destination, and not the journey, Melissa was waiting for her looks to give her the permission she needed – and would never get – to understand the value of what she had to offer from the inside. She was a "No" to her own voice. She sacrificed her own values, instincts, and goals for the passions and expectations of her father. Her allegiance to his vision cost her own.

Now she knows that she already has the prize, and her race is just getting started.

How about you? Do you hear yourself in one of those stories somewhere? How much have you sacrificed already to fulfill another person's vision? How long have you yearned for something that you probably already have, but can't see it clearly? In Kathy Buckley's case, she never even saw a finish line because none of it was ever defined for her – at least not in terms of her prosperity and a clearly defined place in the world of the hearing. For her, the finish line became acceptance and love in a form she would never get – something she was looking outside of herself to find, until she realized that it was there all along, and the one that was cheating her out of it... was her.

If you want a lasting change in how you see your future, here's what you can do about it right now...

CHAPTER ONE HOMEWORK

Get a notebook or a journal. Use this journal as a workbook and tool for your growth and discovery – a reference as you continue to work with this material. Make it as personal and intimate as you want. This will not only be the place for your assignments, but also for you to write down and reflect on thoughts, feelings, fears, and breakthroughs. I've provided space for you to do the exercises in the book as well, but a journal will allow a more complete experience.

Identify three areas in your life where you feel if you didn't have them (i.e. good looks, money, status, fame, etc.), you wouldn't be happy.

1. _____

2. _____

3. _____

Identify the people in your life (i.e. mother, father, siblings, etc.), who you think would be disappointed if you didn't or couldn't achieve the levels of "success" you've identified above.

_____

_____

_____

_____

_____

Ask yourself if this "identity" you possess is really, essentially who you are, or is it something you maintain on a day-to-day basis? If so, who do you feel you really are? Take a moment and describe yourself as you want others to see you, and then how you actually see yourself. Note any differences in the two and why you may have them.

_____

_____

_____

_____

_____

_____

Keep looking back on this work as you progress. We're not at the finish line. We're just getting started and the way to do that is just be an observer. That's it. This will be important later when you do additional homework.

CHAPTER TWO

WHERE WE SELL OUT

In the pursuit of having it all, many of us will sell out a part of ourselves to get it. Being a sell out can appear in the form of lying about your age to get a job or seem more attractive to a mate, abandoning your own personal standards (i.e. diet regimen, honesty principles, doing no harm to others) in order to achieve a goal that ultimately is a "fix" for you anyway.

We all do it. In order to achieve the status we desire, we give up on a previous conversation we have about ourselves that sustained us to that point. For example: "I'll never pose naked just to be famous"; "I'll never marry a man shorter than myself"; "I'll never marry a woman who doesn't work"; "I won't align myself with a faction just to get elected"; "I won't write drivel simply to sell a screenplay." And on and on. At some point in all of our lives, the hunger for what we don't have and so desperately want can make us forget about that moral code, if you will, which already has sustained us.

Think about it... if you've got a negative self-image and you would do anything or accept anything to feel and appear more normal, you are giving up on the standards that you know in your heart are healthy because doing so ultimately reinforces your own self-image of an incomplete person anyway. Melissa in the previous chapter is a perfect example of this. Either way – success by abandoning values, or failure by buying into your own story of being a failure – you lose.

Athletes, business people, politicians, students, mothers, fathers, doctors, and movie stars all share one thing in common in the pursuit of what they have identified as their "goal": At some point they must sacrifice an already existing part of themselves that they value to achieve it.

At some point they sell out.

But it doesn't have to be this way. In this chapter I

provide an example of how easy it is to be a sell-out in order to have a more instant feeling of relevance, and how destructive it can actually be, and a true example of a life lived with purpose, meaning, and relevance without selling out on values.

IDOL FANTASIES

I used to avoid the very popular show *American Idol* until the episodes where they cut all the chafe and goofy contestants and got down to the real competition of actual singing talent. For me, that was when the show truly reached its true possibility. But for those of you who love the entire show – which includes the freak show at the beginning – then you know that there are people who have no sense of self and walk in front of the judges absolutely convinced that indeed they are the next American Idol, all the while painfully unaware of how ridiculous they look. Even worse, some know they look ridiculous, but they just desperately want their fifteen minutes of fame. Or in this case... three minutes.

The point here is that for every one of those blind, tone deaf and DUMB people who have no shot but compete anyway, there are thousands more who never got that far, but still have the same dream: To be famous.

Fame. Why? What is it about the lure of fame that drives a normal human being to seek fame in order to believe that they are more than they are? Well I guess I just answered my own question. But reality has no place in fame, and yet "reality shows" can make the below-average person dumbfoundingly famous.

Now don't get me wrong here... everyone is special in his or her own right, but not everyone is cut out for the spot light.

An example of this occurred in a season not too long ago of American Idol. Apparently two boys appeared on the show hoping that they could find fame and fortune by being "discovered" for their singing talent. One of them was awkwardly short and had a disturbingly odd look on his face. The other was a simple, slow, rather fat kid. Neither of them could sing a note, and both of them were willing to bet their lives that they had what it took for the judges to put them through to the next round. This by the way is nothing new with the show... it has become a staple of the first several weeks to grab ratings.

You can guess what happened... the judges – most notably the sinister but honest Simon Cowell – told both of them they didn't have a chance. But he also made remarks about their appearance, telling one of the boys he looked like a "Bush Baby" and spoke out of the side of his mouth about the other one's large frame.

Needless to say the boys were both shocked and hurt by the rejection, and the comments and left the audition convinced that Simon and his judges were heartless.

The show aired and featured the two boys prominently, and the next day the two boys showed up on *The Today Show* announcing that they had hired agents, and that they were featured on the *Tonight Show* with Jay Leno offering to make them special correspondents to the show's man-on-the-street segment. It seems in fact Simon was perhaps wrong after all, and the boys won!

Nope, sorry. Not so, guys. In fact they lost and they lost badly.

Simon was the only person who was honest with them. He told them what everyone else – including Jay Leno and *The Today Show* was thinking: "These guys are freaks." What they also didn't reveal to the boys was that freaks are fun to look at for a minute, so we're going to get them on the show and expose them to the world. For ratings. Just like American Idol did.

The Today Show didn't feel sorry for those boys. They didn't think they had talent. Jay Leno isn't going to offer them the moon. They are simply extending the opportunity for all us viewer sheep to sit home and smugly laugh at these boys some more. Why? For ratings.

It's exploitation pure and simple, and these two kids are buying into it hook, line, and sinker.

What are they selling out on to be famous? DIGNITY. It's a shame and it makes me mad. Simon Cowell did them a favor. He was honest with them, and instead of listening to the truth, they carried on in their denial of self, and bought in to the temporary wave of fame that would not catapult them into superstardom, but in fact make them a footnote in the annals of geek history, barely registering a worthy mention just a few months later.

Where are they now? Exactly. And what's worse... telling them the truth, or giving them a false promise of fame and stardom, only to rudely yank it away forever when we grow tired of laughing at them, and then turn around to seek out new freaks at which to marvel? I think you know the answer.

The true power is in the acceptance of who you are – and more importantly who you are not – and the ability to not fear that perhaps you are destined to live an "ordinary" life.

And by the way, I don't think that the two guys who competed on American Idol are losers; I simply know that their place in that competition was far different than they intended, or understood. Their greatness will reveal itself to them once they're ready to see it and accept it, and not before.

So is being famous so important, and being ordinary so, well, ordinary? Sometimes being ordinary is noble. Sometimes it means being a stand for other's greatness. Sometimes it means changing the world.

So what does an ordinary life look like, and more importantly, what's so bad about living one? My next subject exemplifies the stoic grace of an ordinary life.

A Legacy of Silent Greatness

My grandfather, Cecil T. Young, lived an average American life in the twentieth Century. He was born in Maynard, Iowa in 1903 and lived ninety-nine years, dying in Oberlin, Ohio in 2003. With the time he was given in between, this son of a Methodist preacher and sibling to five other children married my grandmother and raised three of his own children in and around the mid-western United States. He worked for Northwestern Bell Telephone as a mid-level manager and volunteered with local libraries and his local Methodist church. In his later years during retirement, he brought food to the infirmed through "Meals On Wheels" and stayed interested in politics as much as he was able to tolerate.

The above is everything I knew about my grandfather until the time of his death. It was at his funeral where I learned who my grandfather truly was, and I was proud and surprised to discover a man who helped change the lives of thousands of people in his community, ultimately leaving a legacy of change throughout an entire region of this country.

In the post-war 1950's through to the 1960's, this country saw a boom in just about everything beneficial to Americans. The economy was strong, job opportunities were vast, and babies were being born in record numbers. The American dream was alive and well for nearly everyone in this country.

If you were white.

Cecil, a white middle-class man, was one of the beneficiaries of that great age. But he wasn't content simply taking his slice of the pie and keeping it all to himself. When he lived in Omaha, Nebraska (where he raised my mother), he saw that his community was excluding the opportunity for black families to have affordable, safe housing. Blacks were shuffled to the ghetto region where they were forgotten and, even worse, blamed for their own financial status and other problems. Real estate agents would talk more affluent black families out of moving into exclusive white neighborhoods by telling them it was too expensive, too remote, or anything they could think of to keep the neighborhoods ethnically non-diverse. This was the mid-twentieth century, remember, so this practice was not really frowned upon, nor was it illegal. But it infuriated my grandfather.

He saw the seemingly insurmountable challenges facing black families, and against public and private scrutiny, and he made some noise about it, as was reported in the March 7, 1968 edition of The Omaha *Sun*:

"Cecil T. Young unzipped his case and withdrew a paperback edition of Thornton Wilder's 'ides of March,' the classic about the decline of the Roman Empire. He quoted Julius Caesar: 'But what can I do against the apathy that is glad to wrap itself under the cloak of piety?' The question pretty much summarizes the personal challenge Young sees in his life. It's the challenge of the problem of Negro equality in this country today, a challenge which should be borne high by Christianity, but which the church, according to Young, is failing to meet."

So outraged by the apathy in his community and his own church, Cecil became chairman of the Omaha Presbytery Commission on Religion and Race. He also became a member of the school-community advisory committee to the superintendent of the Omaha Public Schools – a board with which he helped build a strong minority education flavor. This view, sadly, was not too popular, even the mayor, A.V. Sorensen, told him, "I wish I could take this stuff like you do." Generally, the ideas my grandfather promoted were met with reactions of disinterest, unspoken scorn, or a label of "extreme liberal." Ironically, my grandfather was a Republican all his life until the

STOP WAITING FOR PERMISSION!

day he died. And the beauty of his wisdom was that although he embraced a conservative lifestyle, he was after all a man involved in humanity and driven by an unbreakable will to do what was right – not just for himself and his own point of view, but for everyone.

But he couldn't get support from his church to help integrate and support black families, so he joined on with – and helped enhance – Inter-Faith Housing, Inc., a non-profit corporation set up to investigate housing for low and medium-income families under the National Housing Law. Through his efforts and those he inspired, a city block was found, zoned and developed to create multi-family housing for anyone who wanted to live there – black or white.

But he faced severe opposition in the form of protests, petitions and legal action brought by residents of his community, some of whom didn't even live near the planned housing development. But in spite of having no backing from ecumenical, gubernatorial, or residential representatives, my grandfather pushed through the housing development. Several towns mirrored the project, including Topeka, Kansas, to great success.

"The City council will let [this housing initiative] live or die with this case," my grandfather exclaimed. "The council has the opportunity to set Omaha's housing policy. This is a crucial case. If neighborhood pressures can deter our project, they'll be able to do it for anybody else."

Instead of seeing a problem and saying "What are you gonna do?" and forgetting about it, my grandfather stood up and raised his hand—and his voice. And he didn't just point out the problem; he worked to develop solutions based on what he knew in his heart were steps to achieve the goal: Become informed; search out opportunities to know your fellow human beings; contribute time and money to organizations dedicated to helping others; quit telling ethnic jokes; change your mind about your fellow man; write your senators – not just the liberal ones, but the conservatives too – let them know how you feel about the situation; and bring the problem out into the open through organizations you're already a part of.

Within a year of my grandfather's initial efforts, over half the Presbyterian churches in the city and surrounding area subscribed to programs asking suppliers (printers, banks, contractors, any concern dealing in economic transactions with the church) to sign a non-discriminatory pledge.

Now you might think that this part of the story is about how minority families were simply "waiting for permission" to move to a nice area, but no.

The point here is that Cecil didn't need to be a "star" to feel complete in his life. He didn't need fame, fortune, or anything else from anyone else in order to fulfill a purpose he felt was necessary to making life for him and others better. His goal was simple: "Do what is right. Do what is fair." And because of that code, many people for generations after him lived a better life. When he died, he was – for the most part – a true unsung hero. There is a room in the Minnesota Library bearing his name, not because he donated a lot of money, but because of his love for reading, and the impact he had in that community by giving his greatest gift: his heart.

It was one of my goals that my grandfather make it to 100 so Willard Scott could mention him on *The Today Show*. I wanted to the country to know about this wonderful man. Sadly, he died just seven months shy of his centennial. But the works he did to better people's lives have left an indelible legacy. He is a hero to me... A true American Idol.

SWALLOWING MY OWN PILL

In my own struggle to make a difference in life, I have often been hamstrung by the paradigm I set up for myself early in life to achieve success: Revenge. As a host and news reporter, being on television has been a wonderful way to reconnect with old friends who happen to catch me on TV from time to time. (And Facebook is just crazy, ain't it?) It's also been a way to rub my resentment in the face of people in the past that had hurt me in some way or another. My mother would always say to me "Success is the best revenge," and I bought into it, making my career as much about thumbing my nose to past oppressors as having a career I truly loved and in which I excelled.

In a success seminar I attended at Landmark Education in 2004, I learned that old paradigms for success can really make us sell-outs... much like we see all across our culture today, on "American Idol," or any other reality program that has average people dreaming they could be more than they are.

I was taught that the first step to creating a new and powerful paradigm of success was to identify and throw out the old system and create a new one. This wasn't easy, as the old system really served my hunger for success, and I was afraid if I tossed it out, I would have to choose another career.

What I learned was that I didn't have to change a thing about what I wanted, but rather – and quite simply – change the reason I wanted it, and what I could use it for.

So how does a TV host change his reason for wanting to work in television?

The first piece of work involved identifying areas in my life where I previously had great success but never needed acknowledgment or reciprocation. This was easy. About the time my hosting career was taking off, I began to teach hosting classes. I also furthered my love for coaching by getting my certification in hypnotherapy and NLP. I began to find that success for me really came through contribution. I was indeed following in my grandfather's example without knowing it.

Contribution. As the new paradigm of success began to take shape for me, I was also able to let go of all the reasons I had for wanting success in the first place. The new reasons – the reasons that truly suited me – were more than enough.

Here's a true story of what happened at the time I let go of my old paradigm of success:

When I was twenty-one, I had a girlfriend in college – my first real love. We had a pretty typical young relationship, lots of passion – good and bad – and a quick end. But the end was the hard part. We ended very badly, and my heart was truly broken. It took a long time for me to get over her, and very consciously I added her to my revenge list.

Years went by and other relationships came and went, and I eventually got married to an amazing woman, and for the most part I never really thought about her again. But the revenge factor continued to drive my career intensity until the day I let it go for the new paradigm of "Contribution."

One week after completing my success seminar where I created a new paradigm of success, and seventeen years after my college girlfriend and I broke up (without any communication between us that entire time), I got an email from her, completely out of the blue, simply hoping to connect and have final closure for the difficult way we ended things so long ago. One week after I finished the seminar! I'm not kidding. This is a true story.

This example – more than any other – has shown me

that there just might be some force at work that responds to us leaning toward enlightenment and balance. Now don't stand there and say "Okay, I'm enlightened, where's my prize?" That would be focusing on the finish line. Instead really ask yourself if what you're doing to be happy is a fix (i.e. success as revenge) or are you responding to the identification of your own true being?

The epilogue to this story is I didn't even have to quit my career; I simply found a new reason to love it.

When we're a "No" to our own possibilities, we can easily accept "No" for an answer elsewhere from others, or be a "No" to ourselves – ignoring what we know is right – to get what we desire, or simply to be accepted. Here's what to do about that:

CHAPTER TWO HOMEWORK

List three areas in your life where you are a sell-out: Career, relationships, goals, intimacy, etc. Be bold and honest with yourself. This work isn't for the squeamish... you really need to take a bold assessment of yourself. Chances are you already know, which is why you're in this place in your life. List your answers as completely as possible.

1. _____

2. _____

3. _____

Describe in as much detail as you can how, when, and why you sell out in those situations. Ask yourself if selling out in these areas is serving your ultimate goals, or are you simply spinning your wheels? Has being a sell-out helped or hurt your ultimate goal? Ask yourself "Whose life am I living... my parents, my spouse's, my children's? Or mine?" You might want to ask yourself: "Who am I succeeding for?"

_____

_____

_____

_____

_____

_____

_____

PART TWO: PERMISSION

It has been said that luck is preparedness meeting up with opportunity. I can tell you right now that in this current economic stranglehold, there are people just like you – who have never taken risks, made millions, or unveiled a new innovation – but who right now are taking this moment to create something from nothing. Be it desperation or inspiration, they are motivated not only by the opportunities (and they're out there), but by understanding what they have to offer.

One of the most poignant quotes I've ever heard comes from Nelson Mandela: "Our deepest fear is not that we are inadequate. Our deepest fear is that we are powerful beyond imagination. It is our light more than our darkness which scares us. We ask ourselves – who are we to be brilliant, beautiful, talented, and fabulous. But honestly, who are you to not be so?"

Don't fear your gifts. Don't protect them. Use them now, because someone else is going to invent that really cool thing you thought of a year ago, but they're going to develop it, register it, and take it to market. Will you be banging your head against the wall a year from now because you didn't follow through on "The Tummy Terminator"?

And if it's love you're protecting yourself from, or looking for in the wrong places, sit for a moment and ask yourself if holding back really serves the other person who is losing out on you and your greatness. You have to stop looking for love, and start looking for all the barriers within yourself that you have put up against it.

It's easy to play small, not risking anything, but if you fail without trying, you deserve it. If you fail while taking a risk, then you can learn from it, and that is when anything is possible.

At the end of the day I'd rather go to bed exhausted from trying than exhausted from feeling like a failure.

In the first section of the book, I introduced you to some amazing people who faced adversity and sought out a different and new way of life for the better. Believe it or not, you are one of them. In this next section, it is my intention that you get for yourself not only a better sense of who you are and what you want, but also an understanding that, until now, just "wanting more" was not enough. True prosperity, growth, change, and happiness come from allowing yourself to take the new steps necessary to move forward and more importantly, *allowing* the prosperity to respond. If you've got the ability but don't use it, you'll never have what you deserve. If you want it, but push it away when it shows up, then you've got to look at why you want it in the first place.

Let's see how much good you actually allow in your life.

CHAPTER THREE
THE RACE

- OR -

WHAT A CAMERAMAN TAUGHT ME ABOUT THE MYTH OF UTOPIA

GROUND RULES

Several years ago I was hosting a show for a cable network where we would go to people's houses and get them started in the process of re-landscaping their yards. On every show I ever worked, there were the usual cast of characters: hair and makeup crew, lighting guys, producers, production assistants, sound crew, and of course the camera operators. (They prefer to be called DP's – Directors of Photography)

One average day during an average taping of an average show, while we were having our usual lunch break, the crew and I got into a very unusual discussion. Instead of the usual quotes from *Monty Python's Flying Circus* or *Zoolander* or *Anchorman*, we somehow got on the subject of politics. It was an election year, so I suppose that had something to do with it.

I brought up my usual rants about how a corrupt government where only the top have control and everyone else is squashed down is ruining all that our founding fathers intended for us. I went on about how if every person in this country, indeed this world, were enlightened, we wouldn't need leaders! We would all be powerful, strong, self-governing. The need for society as we live it now wouldn't be necessary.

Sitting across from me was the cameraman for the shoot that day. Usually during the day's lunches, he was quiet. Not rude, he just never really got into the conversations. I just always thought he was just not a talker. But after a few thoughtful seconds, he put down his sandwich and quietly remarked that if indeed all of us in society were leaders, there would be chaos.

He said, "The way societies truly work is through a leader-follower scenario. Since the earliest man, someone has stepped up to lead, and the rest have followed."

And here's the kicker that blew me away... he continued:

"And that's the way most people want it. They want to follow. They want to be led. In fact, they don't mind being lied to as long as they get to keep what they have."

That little slice of insight floored me. It only took me a moment to wrap my mind around it, but I realized he was absolutely right.

MY WEEK ON A JURY

Years later, I experienced that precise scenario when I served on a jury for a week. The case was simple; a young lady who was shopping late at night at a discount store was injured when some highly stacked boxes fell on her. It was a quick trial and the case was given to us within four days.

As we walked into the jury room for the first time to begin deliberating, I was eager to see if anyone on the jury would take what was obviously the foreman's chair at the end of the long table. Slowly, we all filed in; I made sure I was the last one. I wanted to see if there were any leaders (beside myself) who would take the seat.

Honestly, I was hoping to be the foreman, but I was willing to give that up to see the results of my experiment. And guess what... NO ONE SAT IN THE SEAT! They all looked at each other, and then at me, waiting for someone to lead them.

It was fascinating to me to see this unfold. As we all sat down, no one spoke. They all looked at me. So I asked, "Who wants to be the foreman? Do we have a foreman?" feigning confusion. They looked at one another, and then at me until one person said, "I thought you were." The rest of the people agreed in what seemed like the immediate release of mutual tension, and with that little assignment behind us, we were under way.

I accepted the foreman position mainly because I love to lead. But I soon found that leading this group of 11 others was difficult. Not because we disagreed, or because they rebelled against my leadership, but because they simply laid down and allowed me to make the decisions, come to conclusions, and assign punishment to the defendant. For less than two days we talked about the case and rarely would any of the other jurors propose ideas, argue opposing theories, or question the process.

And believe me, I'm being completely honest when I tell you that as foreman I insisted that everyone participate speak, theorize, and judge. But it was like pulling teeth with most of them.

There was one gentleman, interestingly the only other male in the group, who occasionally stated that he felt the plaintiff deserved more money than we were thinking about awarding. I was so relieved to have another voice in the room. But, because my individual argument was for slightly less money, the rest of the jurors sided with me in the voting, and I'm convinced it was simply because I was the leader.

In the end I got everything I wanted out of the process. The money awarded the plaintiff was exactly what I thought was fair. Ten others went along, the eleventh juror – the only other man – succumbed, and we were done before dinner on Friday.

Because it was a jury situation and not a scientific experiment, I really didn't feel comfortable polling the others about their roles as members of our panel. But after spending a week with them, I can tell you that what came across for me was clear: Most of us in this life will abdicate, or worse, never seek to lead, and thus never get what they want. The one guy who tried to have a say got overruled, not because the rest of the jury didn't agree with him, but because he never assumed leadership and lost the opportunity to have a strong voice.

The caveat to all of this is that other guy on the jury might have been right. Maybe the plaintiff did deserve more money. I hope that my case was unique, rather than the norm, but I fear it may not be. I believe my experience on that jury proved exactly the theory that the cameraman espoused years earlier.

ON YOUR MARK, GET SET...

The Olympics. Field day. Two sprinters wait at the starting line. Thousands of fans in the stands. The man with the starting gun fires the gun. The runners take off. At the end of the race, the two runners cross the line and break the tape together. The picture is inconclusive. It's up the judges to make the call.

You're one of the runners.

Who has the power?

How you answer that question tells a lot about how you view the world and your place in it, don't you think?

Let's imagine you say, "Well, logically, the judges have the power. They make the final decision, and the runners by agreement must abide by that ruling. Clearly the judges are the ones in this situation with the power."

Or you might say: "I'm an enlightened person... I can choose to run or not run, and I can choose to accept the judges' decision or not. I have choice in all things, so clearly I have the power."

Either answer would indicate that you are a person who is aware of the world and how you fit in it. People live and die every day in the world, and between those two events they usually do the best they can to work within a set of organized parameters they have come to understand as "That's just the way it is."

So where do you think the power is? With the judges, or with yourself?

Before you answer, remember that there was a third element in the story. Remember?

Remember the man with the starting gun? What if I told you that the man with the starting gun actually had the power? While you are waiting to start, nervously, anxiously, you know you can't do a thing until that gun goes off. Certainly the judges can't judge you until you are in motion and cross the finish line, and if you were to have a "false start," you would have to start over or be disqualified.

The man with the gun. Not what you were expecting? The good news is that in this hypothetical story, and for the purposes of this book, all the characters – the two runners, the judges and the man with the gun – are actually all facets of you. The race is the struggle you have each day to accomplish all of your "wants."

So what do you want, and why don't you have it? Chances are you're doing everything you can NOT to accomplish your goals. Really. Shocked? Are you one of those people who need to be lied to as long as you have your piece of the pie and just simply get along in life? I don't think so. There is something better available for you; otherwise, you wouldn't spend your time wishing you had it.

True, as a society, we need our leaders to do the things for us we don't have the time, talent, interest, ability or passion, to do. So we accept our roles as followers. And that's fine. After all we can't all be leaders, right?

But somewhere between the understanding of society's social structure and your own life, there is a disconnect. You've become powerless in areas where you are perfectly able to have the power.

Remember Melissa and her dad? She realized her own power to accept herself as she was in deference to what she thought her father would appreciate. How about the guy on the jury with me? There's no power in judging yourself or others as being inferior – especially where looks are involved, or where you fear to lead.

FRANK AND GAIL ZAPPA

Say what you want about Frank Zappa, and that's exactly what he wanted you to do – to have the freedom to express yourself however you wish.

Most people who know of Frank Zappa know him as an outrageous musician whose extremely "colorful" lyrics and song subjects left many censors screaming to ban his music.

I grew up listening to Zappa albums with my older brother, laughing hysterically at his hilarious songs with titles like "Broken Hearts Are For Assholes," "Nanook Rubs It," "Flakes," Tittles and Beer," "Bobby Brown," and the more well known songs "Jewish Princess," "Dancing Fool," and "Valley Girl." His rock opera "Joe's Garage" remains one of the most influential and unique musical influences in my life.

But Zappa didn't just write and record albums that made the parents of 1970's and 1980's pre-teens cringe. He was also an extremely accomplished and celebrated modern music composer. His work, "London Symphony Orchestra, Vol. 1," contained orchestral compositions conducted by Kent Nagano and performed by the London Symphony Orchestra. A second record of these sessions, "London Symphony Orchestra, Vol. 2," released in 1987, had reviewers noting that the recordings were the best representation of Zappa's orchestral work.

Because of backlash to his controversial lyrics, Zappa also became a staunch defender of the First Amendment and gave a new meaning to "Free Speech" by pointing out that words should not have the power to harm or shock people. They are after all just words, Zappa would argue.

On September 19, 1985, Zappa testified before the U.S. Senate Commerce, Technology, and Transportation committee, attacking the Parents Music Resource Center or PMRC, a music organization, co-founded by then-Senator Al Gore's wife, Tipper. Consisting of many wives of politicians, including the wives of five members of the committee, the PMRC was founded to address the issue of song lyrics with sexual or "satanic" content. Zappa saw the writing on the wall: this was leading to censorship, and he called their proposal for voluntary labeling of records with explicit content "extortion" of the music industry. In his prepared statement, he said:

"The PMRC proposal is an ill-conceived piece of nonsense which fails to deliver any real benefits to children, infringes the civil liberties of people who are not children, and promises to keep the courts busy for years dealing with the interpretational and enforcemental problems inherent in the proposal's design. It is my understanding that, in law, First Amendment issues are decided with a preference for the least restrictive alternative. In this context, the PMRC's demands are the equivalent of treating dandruff by decapitation ... The establishment of a rating system, voluntary or otherwise, opens the door to an endless parade of moral quality control programs based on things certain Christians do not like. What if the next bunch of Washington wives demands a large yellow *J* on all material written or performed by Jews, in order to save helpless children from exposure to concealed Zionist doctrine?"

Zappa set excerpts from the PMRC hearings to Synclavier music in his composition "Porn Wars" on the 1985 album "Frank Zappa Meets the Mothers of Prevention." Zappa is heard interacting with Senators Fritz Hollings, Slade Gorton, Al Gore (who admitted to being a Zappa fan), and in an exchange with Florida Senator Paula Hawkins over what toys Zappa's children played with.

Zappa went on to argue with PMRC representatives on CNN's Crossfire in 1986 – and incendiary discussion that you must see! (Check it out on YouTube).

Zappa's passion for American politics was becoming a bigger part of his life. He had always encouraged his fans to register to vote on album covers, and throughout 1988 he had registration booths at his concerts. He even considered running for president of the United States.

Without a doubt, Frank Zappa's rock albums are not for everyone, nor are his modern music compositions. But there is no doubt that the man who created the music that many believe was far ahead of his time was a man of principle and a firm believer in the freedoms allowed us in the Constitution, and ultimately as conscious, intelligent beings.

When I began this book, deciding to feature pioneers who exemplify not taking "No" for an answer, Frank was one of the first on my list. Because of his death in 1994, I obviously could not have been able to interview him, but I was generously invited to his home by his wife, Gail, to speak with her about Frank.

Their house, nestled in the hills above Los Angeles, is a hidden-away, unassuming place that is easy to miss due to a large amount of foliage adorning the outer gate near the street entrance. Warm and inviting, it is loaded with countless artifacts saturating the walls, coffee tables, and desks, chronicling the life and activities of Frank Zappa. Everywhere I turned I found a unique moment in not only Frank's life, but also my own memories as a fan.

Gail met me in the main office, just offset from the music studio where Frank composed and recorded many of his albums. Two of their four children, Ahmet and Diva (Moon Unit and Dweezil were out of town), passed through the room at various times during the interview, busily attending to the family business: Maintaining the legacy, and re-introducing the works and deeds of their father. It was also the house where Frank died, surrounded by his family. I was keenly aware of the completeness of the experience and often found myself in disbelief that I was actually in the home of one of my earliest influences... an influence that ultimately would lead to this book.

As an interviewer and reporter, I prided myself over the years in creating a great first question that would launch a conversation with my subject, rarely working from prepared questions. In this case, I didn't get that far. I simply sat down with Gail and asked the first thing that came to my mind. The rest was what follows.

What made you fall in love with Frank Zappa?

(laughs) You want the real answer! OK, I can't isolate one single thing, but I can tell you what cemented it. When I really understood this was the real deal and that was the guy for me - then everything fell into place absolutely. It was a story that he told me. And that's when I knew, there's nobody else like him. The story was... there was this couple, and when they went to bed they closed the door to the bedroom and got into bed and went to sleep. Suddenly they heard this noise that woke them up, so the guy gets up and he turns on the light and there's this monster in the room! There was a noise that he made that sort of went along with it...sort of a horrible, kind of slurpy, hideous noise. And the guy says, "How'd that get in here?"

And that's when I realized, OK, no one would say that, only [Frank] would say, how did that get in here. It has nothing to do with, what are you going to do now, there's a monster, what's it going to do to you, is it dangerous? Can it hurt you, is it going to melt your face, I mean what's it going to do? But that's not your consideration; your concern is how did that get in here. Like, how did these conditions come together?

It's just natural curiosity…

It's total natural curiosity and it's funny, because he's totally stepped outside of it…like the man in the story is not concerned about his own welfare, or for anything else. Just wants to know what the deal is in terms of the universe. You know? (laughs)

And that was it for you?

That was it.

Because it was his mind, the way he thought.

Yeah.

Were you thinking that way?

I have no idea. I don't know how I think, I just know what I think, but I don't know how I think. I just know that it's a whole lot of fun and it took me a long time to figure out that thinking is actually, really, really fun. And if you can put aside all the crap that isn't about thinking, it is possible to have such a great time.

So, what I was saying is, People that I think are recognized as visionaries are actually people who can see the greatest…who have the ability to perceive pattern recognition across time and space…in a huge way. It's like, if you imagine that most people can fit what's on the breakfast table in front of them inside their head, that's all they really imagine, that they can deal with inside their head, but other people are capable of putting the entire universe, the entire known and the potential for the unknown inside their head, and those people that can do that can see huge patterns across all the information that that contains. And if you can recognize patterns, you can predict the outcome of certain types of events. And those people are visionaries.

Like Frank?

Yes.

When Frank was on Crossfire in 1986 and he's getting it from both sides in a way, but really from that one guy, he seemed to be exhibiting what you're talking about. He was saying, "What I'm talking about is the big picture." A leadership which is coming dangerously close to a theocracy, which was so prophetic, in terms of what's happening now, and...

But everything was already in place for that to happen...

The Reagan years?

Yeah. That's when it started, pretty much.

He warned of the theocracy taking over and he also fought, obviously, very hard for the abolition of censorship for music...

The aspect of censorship that he was discussing was that unlike other forms of commercial...things that are registered as commercial products, by parents who are purchasing them for their children, such as films and that sort of thing, music is usually made by one person. A song is written by one or two people. And then it's performed by an artist, so that if you are going to censor Frank Zappa, for example, you're censoring that person. As a society, you're saying that person doesn't have a right to speak. That person doesn't have a right to exist, that person doesn't have a right to express his opinions because he's obscene. And that's where that was going, because when PMRC originally asked for the record industry to consider labeling records, the labels they wanted were: O for obscene,

V for violent, and the like. It's like the list that they published of all the artists whose music should be considered dangerous. Everybody on the list was black...on the one that they first published and they immediately yanked that when we brought that to their attention. But they're alluding to the fact that they're dangerous to the minds of the youth right? Because they are affecting children, you know. So one minute you're a child at seventeen and you can't buy ...I don't know... like Def Leppard or even Prince without your parents' permission and the next minute, you turn eighteen, they stick a gun in your hand and send you to war. None of it makes sense... We're talking about rights that are guaranteed whether you've hit the age of 'maturity' or not, in terms of what ideas you're allowed to hear. Like it's freedom to read, freedom to listen to the music of your choice, and especially, as far as Frank is concerned, it is the First Amendment. Now, it's not set aside specifically for artists' rights to express themselves, it's just guaranteed under the Constitution of the United States, which also guarantees copyrights, by the way, that you have the right, as an artist or as a citizen to freedom of speech. That's the deal.

What got him so passionate about this in the first place?

His entrapment and arrest when he was a young man?

I don't think that that worked that way for Frank. Frank Zappa was the most present person I have ever known in my life. Most people who are carrying around the great burden of the effects of things that have happened to them and all the bad stuff that they have to put up with... they are dealing in the past, they are bringing whatever they are hurting last Tuesday, or when they were three, forward into the present and still nurturing it. OK, that means these people are living in the past. They're fucked up. Then there's the people that are just dreaming of how things will be and these are the people that are more often known as waiting for their life to occur. They're living in a future that they are not participating in and they're sad, you know, in the present, because they can't be in the future. Well, the past is over, and the future never will happen. Everything is always now. Pay attention, if you want to have a great time, no matter what, stay fixed in reality because there's no one there to bother you. Because reality is a place where the egos don't live, they don't thrive, they don't work really well. And once you get past all that stuff, that's when thinking is really fun.

When I was in college, I was watching Arsenio Hall and Frank was on. Arsenio was pumping up the band, he was saying, "Whoa you're so great, you're so awesome" and they'd go off to commercial and they'd go back and he'd say, "Thanks band, you're the greatest band I ever heard" and Frank finally said, "Well if they're so great, why don't you let them play during the show?" And Arsenio just didn't even know what to do. He didn't know how to respond, so he retorted with an insult at Frank for calling him out: "Yeah, they might be better than some of the musical guests we have on the show." Frank didn't even flinch, he knew he had the edge and it was so present... perfect.

Well, that is typical Frank Zappa. He asked the questions that no one else bothers to ask. That's because he could really think. And he's an observer.

What gave him the permission to say everything he felt like saying ... where did it come from?

A lot of re-wiring, which was internal work on himself, by himself. But , first it's a natural curiosity that led him to the larger questions, and being able to evaluate them in a larger context with a larger purpose, so I think that the answer to the question really is freedom. Freedom gave him permission. You want to choose freedom... you can't go anyplace else, there's no place else to go. Frank often said, 'I am limited by my own freedom.'

If freedom gave him permission, how was he limited by it?

Because if you only choose freedom, that's all you can ever do.

You can't go back.

You can't go sideways, you can't go up, down, away or through, that is the constant choice, that is like the price of freedom, like Thomas Jefferson said, "The price of freedom is eternal vigilance."

The price becomes a burden, doesn't it?

It is a burden...

When he was in Congress and he was obviously using the hatred of the way things were to fight for free speech, what was he like when he came back from testimony? What was his reaction, how do you feel it landed for him?

He didn't evaluate it in terms of himself. That's the thing that people don't realize. This is not a career move. He's objective. He predicted what it was going to be. You can see it in the statements that he made. He knows what people are thinking about this particular topic and he's just hoping...Frank believed that you couldn't change anybody's mind. Everybody's so concerned with themselves and their relation to the universe, and how things affect them and nobody's looking out for anybody else.

It's no different than when you play a piece of music. There's information embedded in the music, just in the structural aspect of the music, and you're introducing people to sounds that they've never heard before or you know, mathematical structures that they're not familiar with and that opens their minds up for other possibilities. So, the way that you speak is an act of composition and you're hoping to catch the people that might just say, OK, you know what? There's something going on there that I didn't really recognize before. And maybe that will spark the imagination of the person that manages to hear that. You know, and then maybe they'll wake up. Some part of them will wake up and they'll realize what is at stake is freedom always and democracy is a great fucking idea founded on the principles that, of recognizing, I mean of people who understand democracy and how important an idea it is, know that it's founded on freedom.

Speaking of democracy, what he would do at his shows is he would register people to vote.

He is one of the first people to do that in the concert venues, yeah, through the able assistance of the League of Women's Voters. That's how they did it. *Rolling Stone* reported that other people were doing it, but he'd already registered about 11,000. That doesn't seem like a very large number, but I think in those days it was.

He said also, you know, if you don't like the way thing are, vote. If you don't like the leaders, run for something.

Yeah, he was going to run for president.

You're kidding.

No, he was ready to...oh yeah, but then he was diagnosed with cancer, which was incurable, at the stage that he was diagnosed, but for two years nobody knew that.

Did he choose to die?

I think he probably did.

Why?

It's what he wanted on his tombstone, which I refused to put the tombstone up.

He has an unmarked grave.

That's right he does, and I've never told anybody this but, he said, "If you ever choose to put a headstone, I want it to say, 'too little, too late.' That's why I believe it.

If everyone in the world was like Frank, can you imagine such a world?

I think that if everybody in the world was like Frank, Frank would be intensely bored.

And back to the topic of "No?"

It's one thing to not take "No" for an answer, but the best way to be able to be in a position to do that, and I suspect if you ask some other people, they'd tell you this too, in order to do that, you have to understand the word "No." It's not everybody who gets to own and operate that thing. You have to know what it means and that is the one thing that I usually say that I learned best from Frank... is how to earn and operate the word No. "No" means you are willing to walk away. There is a point beyond which you will not go. If you can do that, then you understand it. Most people will threaten "No," but they never mean it. Frank Zappa was the guy that meant it. When he said "No," it was "No," clearly. He would walk away. I don't care how much money was involved, I don't care what was at stake, there's a point at which, as an artist or as a human being, he recognized he's not going to cross that line and then that's when you know that "No" belongs to you. Then you can control it. Once it belongs to you, you own it forever.

• • •

For the record, it took me nearly a year to get the interview with Gail. Many requests were ignored or denied, not because of any sense of grandeur on her part, but I really believe that she was testing me to see if I was walking my talk – actually not taking "No" for an answer – and her eventual acceptance email to me reflected that. Of all of the people I have met and interviewed over the years, this experience will remain as one of the best for me. I thank Gail very much for letting me in.

It seems to me, as I get older, that life prepares you for life. The things we learn in our youth create the network of responses, understandings, and reactions for our future. The best of us will tell you that they're still learning lessons 40, 50, 60 years into their lives, and they are completely fascinated by their ongoing discoveries. If all we have to rely upon is one set of instructions upon which we spend our lives following, and suddenly one day the rules change, imagine the confusion and pain brought on by that reality. This is why child stars have so much trouble acclimating to an adult life where the word "No" is heard perhaps for the first time. You wonder why so many of them take to drugs. For them, and for those blessed with beauty, life can be a cold hard slap in the face when they are no longer valued for the things they grew up counting on.

There is a wonderful quote, which I used earlier in the book, that states: "When challenged or in a crisis, you don't rise to the level of the situation, you sink to the level of your training!" For military and police, that statement strikes a poignant chord. But for the rest of us, it still makes sense if you apply it to how we live our lives every day. Who you are in the face of adversity says a lot about whom you chose to be *before* the adversity showed up.

Remember the race. It all starts with the gun. Remember too that somewhere between the understanding of society's social structure and your own life, there is a disconnect. You've become powerless in areas where you are perfectly able to have the power. Being fully loaded with your own resources – possessing a complete understanding of who you are, with every resource ready and available to you at any given moment – will help you in the scenarios outlined in the next chapter.

Being a "No" to all of our opportunities for growth and understanding can create crippling effects in our lives for years. Don't forget that the mirror only shows you what you need to see. Good or bad! The homework in this chapter will help that.

CHAPTER THREE HOMEWORK

Identify at least three areas in your life where you apologize, shrink or check out when you feel your greatness might offend or put someone off. What do you do?

1. _____

2. _____

3. _____

Remember a situation from your past – a specific moment – where you held back because you thought someone might feel less of himself or herself because of who you were being. What did you do? Do you regret it?

_____

_____

_____

_____

_____

_____

_____

Dig really deep and remember a time when you denied yourself the possibility of being your best because it felt "too good" or "foreign" and so you held back. Describe that event. How did you feel after you held back... relieved or sad?

_____

_____

_____

_____

Answer the following questions. "Who am I?" "What do I want?" "Who am I not?" "What don't I want?" Start with a paragraph or two. Write as much as you feel like writing in response to each question. Describe everything about you that you know, feel, suspect or think you don't know! Have fun with the exercise: it's designed to get you thinking about yourself in a complete way.

_____

_____

_____

_____

_____

CHAPTER FOUR

THE MOST POWERFUL WORD IN THE WORLD

No

For all of us that word can be a blessing or a curse, a command or a challenge, a liberator, or a killer. What is it for you?

For me (often to my wife's frustration), "No" is rarely an option. In the case of writing this book, it has been a liberating thing. Many of my interview subjects told me "No" – some a dozen times – before finally agreeing to talk with me. Nothing personal, I just had to prove I wanted it. My one big prize, Arnold Schwarzenegger, however, continued to elude me to point where I honestly believed even I could not get the interview. More on that later.

The thing that confounds me today is that most people who *are* in a position to help you (customer service personnel and the like) are the first people to tell you "No" when you have a need.

There was a great commercial a little while back starring David Spade for Capital One where people call him all day asking to redeem their credit card miles and his answer is always NO. That series of commercials makes great sport of what I consider to be a real problem in our culture: We just don't have the time or the interest to help anyone anymore. Well, the truth is we do, we really just don't want to.

And that's unacceptable.

MAY I PLEASE SPEAK TO YOUR SUPERVISOR?

Whenever I've got a customer service need – an issue with some product that needs to be resolved – I call the customer service number listed and as soon as I can navigate through the endless network of automated responses, (just press zero a lot, that will get you through fast), and get a real person on the phone, I simply and politely insist on talking to their manager, supervisor, or boss. And I keep asking. I don't take "No" for an answer. The Verizon situation I talk about in a moment tells it all.

Look, the people hired to answer the phones and take care of your requests deal with people like you all day long. They hear complaint after complaint after complaint, and honestly they really don't have any power to affect any real change. I'm not saying everyone who is a customer service professional is like David Spade at Capital One, but usually the results are the same: "Sorry, but I can't help you."

Last year my cellular phone carrier jacked up my rates by twenty percent and limited my call time by thirty percent. This was after four years of being a loyal customer and always paying my bill on time. On top of that, they weren't interested in compensating my dismay with an upgraded phone! The worst part was that they never bothered to tell me they were doing any of this. I just noticed one month that my bill had doubled! So I got on the phone (my home phone) and believe me... After a painstaking navigation through countless button options and several attempts by the reps to get me to NOT talk to the boss, I got through to the boss's boss! I let her know exactly how unhappy I was with this sudden turn of events and "I'm sorry there's nothing we can do" just wasn't going to cut it.

By the time I was off the phone, I got my minutes back up to where they were. I still had an increase in rates, (that was a nation-wide staple), but within the next two days I received – free – the top of the line newest phone they had to offer.

Just recently, my wife and I moved, and we relied upon many different services to make the process hassle-free, including phone transfer, mail transfer, paint and construction workers, appliance delivery services, trash removal, electrical, plumbing and gas contractors, moving company, and satellite TV installation. Of everyone I just mentioned, the only people we didn't have problems with were the moving company. In every other instance – and believe me I could write an entire book about just this moving experience – each company or contractor hired and paid by us delivered service anywhere between bad and "I can't believe they are still in business!" kind of service. The company I'll focus on is our phone company, Verizon, without a doubt the worst company I have ever encountered in terms of customer service. From the indecipherable and apathetic outsourced customer service reps to the indifferent company managers, this company never once got my service needs correct. For nine days I spoke on the phone with perhaps up to fifteen different managers – not customer service agents, but their bosses – trying to figure out why the didn't transfer my service, why they cancelled my email, and why it was so hard to remedy. It took me nine days. Why? I was transferred and hung up on at least twenty-five times. I was told at least eight times there was nothing they could do. Nothing they could do? It's their business to connect me! Have you seen those commercials? That's all they do! The level of incompetence was so bad I began to actually think I was being punk'd! Really! I have never experienced such a nightmare. The issue, which could have been resolved in one day, took over a week to solve because no one in the company got invested in my problem. They all wanted to pass the buck, blame another department, put me on hold, whatever. Not one customer service agent truly served me as a customer.

Finally, one month after moving, all my services were restored but I got the most outrageous bill -- $432 – for services I had to use because of their mistake. I got back on the phone and for another two days spoke with high-level managers only, and got $320 taken off the bill. All the waiting on hold, the hang-ups and the frustration was worth it because in the end I got what I wanted and what I deserved. And in the end, whether I saved money or not, I didn't take "No" for an answer, I stood up for my interests and got what I deserved.

There is an unspoken deal we have with those who are in a position to help us that we'll ask for a refund, or a return, or a better room, or a better airplane seat, and the answer is usually "No." And we accept that answer with the attitude of "Hey what are you gonna do, I tried?" And that's supposing that you even tried in the first place! Well I suppose that attitude is alright with customer service if you really don't care that you can't return your brand new microwave, but what about when you ask your leaders to protect your interests and the answer is "No". Do you just say "Hey, what are you gonna do"? The answer to that question today I'm afraid is often yes.

We have come to expect less from our leaders and anyone else who provides a service, either public or private. And so the desire for taking a stand for getting what you want or what you deserve gets lost in the apathy created by the fear that what you already have will be taken away if you fight for what you want.

As of this edition, a change is occurring in our leadership. Our new president, Barack Obama ("Yes we can!"), is seeking to responsibly and adroitly end the conflict in Iraq. We were misled into that war, and told to stay there for no reason and without any sacrifice – the two things Americans understand: Reasons and Sacrifice. The difference in policy toward the Iraq war and war in Vietnam is simple: The Vietnam War saw huge anti-war sentiment because there was a draft in place. The stakes were higher for those who were eligible to fight. If your number was called, you either shipped out or headed north to Canada. Those who opposed the draft but stayed were imprisoned. Of course there were riots! Kent State is a perfect example of the kind of fever Americans felt when they actually had something to lose. Today most of us continue to live our comfortable lives while "others" fight for us. Imagine the uproar if there were a draft in place today! Things would be a lot different, wouldn't they?

But with the current state of the economy, it seems we've all been drafted into a different kind of war against the outrageous practices of those who were supposed to have our best interests in mind. There have been many casualties and losses and a lot of fog and confusion about how to handle the problem. It seems that in this time of extinction and rebirth that, now more than ever, the people have the say as to how we shall overcome. The people. You and me. Perhaps we can all be leaders and have a voice after all?

For some throughout history, taking "No" for an answer was simply not an option. These have been ordinary people like you and me who saw a wrong and stood up and said "I think that the way things are going are not good, and I'm tired of asking you for change. Now I'm going to make it happen my self." Those are the men and women who have shaped our history – and not all of them have been our leaders.

BURT RUTAN

One of my personal heroes is Burt Rutan, the designer of "SpaceShip One," the first private craft to reach space, perform a sub-orbital arc, and return safely. This resulted in his winning the Ansari X-Prize and partnering with Virgin Galactic to create the first space-liner! I've been a long-time fan of Mr. Rutan since my early sailing days. As a kid, I spent several summers on our boat with my dad and brother criss-crossing the North Atlantic near Newport, Rhode Island to catch a glimpse of the America's Cup yachts as they raced.

One year there was a great upheaval in the racing community when the New Zealand team challenged the racing establishment with an entirely new design of boat. It was a catamaran, and up until then *all* America's Cup challenge boats were standard, single-hulled vessels measuring twelve meters long. This fast innovation used a wing for its only sail. A wing! I remember thinking then, despite my father's outrage at the audacity of the Kiwis, that not only was the design fresh, but the thought of using a wing to propel a boat through the water was mind boggling. Years later I discovered that the designer of that concept was Burt Rutan, and ever since I have followed his career with great enthusiasm. He has yet to disappoint.

Rutan was an aircraft aficionado from the start. He was designing and building model aircraft by the time he was eight years old. At sixteen he performed his first solo flight in an old Aeronca Champ tail dragger, and by the time he was twenty-two, he graduated third in his class from Cal-Tech with an aeronautical engineering degree.

For the next ten years, Rutan worked for the U.S. Air Force at Edwards Air Force Base as a flight test project engineer, and as director of the Bede Test Center for Bede Aircraft, in Newton, Kansas.

In 1974, at the age of twenty-nine, Rutan struck out on his own and created the Rutan Aircraft Factory in the Mojave Desert, where he designed and developed homebuilt prototypes for a number of aircraft, mostly based on his own radical designs. One of the more recognizable features of a Rutan-designed plane is the forward canard. A canard is like a small wing, maybe the size of a tail wing, which Rutan placed in the front of most of the fuselage, now a standard feature for a Rutan-designed plane.

In April 1982, Rutan founded Scaled Composites, which has become one of the world's pre-eminent aircraft design and prototyping facilities.

Rutan designed Voyager, the first plane to fly around the world without stopping or refueling. That plane now hangs in the Milestones of Flight exhibit in the National Air and Space Museum, sharing space with the Wright Flyer and Charles Lindbergh's Spirit of St. Louis.

But it seems, thankfully, that the sky was not the limit for Burt Rutan. Fueled by frustration with NASA bureaucracy, a passion for space travel and the call of the Ansari X-Prize (a contest awarding 10-million dollars to the first private sub-orbital space flight), Rutan set out to design and build "SpaceShip One," which made its record-breaking, news-making flight in October of 2004, and which also now hangs in the National Air and Space Museum in Washington D.C. The achievement was instantly commercialized as Richard Branson and Virgin Galactic swooped down to partner with Rutan to create "SpaceShip Two," the first tourist space ship ever.

My conversation with Rutan was both predictable and surprising at the same time – predictable, in that I knew his feelings about innovation and what he sees as the stagnancy of NASA, but surprising in his openness about his own personal history, thoughts, and dreams. The conversation lasted about twenty minutes (he promised me only five) and his soft, thought-filled cadence at times made it seem as though he was designing the newest, as yet un-seen space craft while talking with me over the phone from his headquarters in the desert.

In terms of taking "No" for an answer how do you avoid that?

Well, if you know you're right, you can always say "No" back.

So you're saying "No" is a good thing to say?

In my case, yes

How so?

With government regulators, for example. We were regulated for our space flights by a portion of the FAA that doesn't work with airplanes. They only work with expendable missiles. The Office of Commercial Space Transportation only licensed delta and atlas rockets that were used to launch commercial satellites and such, and I showed up with an airplane to do a space flight and insisted that I be regulated by the part of the FAA that understands airplanes. It was totally different than a computer-guided missile, which is indeed very dangerous. And an airplane is indeed very reliable, or they wouldn't let you fly it. Several times during the process I said no to being regulated by the Office of Commercial Space Transportation. I didn't win all the battles, but I won most of them.

How have you won those battles?

Again, it's just that if you know you're right, you're basically going to win, so you stand up in front and say no! I call it the Nancy Reagan approach, you know, "Just say no!"

Why is there so much apathy in the world of innovation?

Because, in many ways, people take the easy way.

Who does that serve?

The best example I can think of is NASA, as a research and development organization. They did phenomenally historic, excellent research in the 60's... Alan Shepard flew a sub-orbital space flight... our first astronaut, and 10 years later he was golfing on the moon! That kind of progress and breakthrough is truly research. Now contrast that to what's going on now with our attempt to go back to the moon. I make the point that there's no research at all – it's all development. Because they're taking things that they know work... pieces from the shuttle and Saturn V, and putting them together and technically it's boring. It's not research. They're precluding the opportunity to have a breakthrough that will help us get to mars. That's something that should be done by a businessman who wants to mine the moon; he doesn't want to take any risks or learn anything new... that would be his approach, he could to go to the parts bin and put pieces together so he can go to the moon to mine the minerals that he wants to mine.

But NASA – who is using tax payer's dollars for research – should go back to the moon again. It should do so by learning new breakthroughs that will help us get to the moons of Saturn where we know there is the possibility of water. A lot of people say I'm a NASA critic, and I don't appreciate the neat things NASA has done. That's not true at all. I'm awed by them, but I think they should not do what they're doing now.

You mean the ARES rockets; NASA's proposed vehicles to get us back to the moon?

Yeah... let the Chinese go back to the Apollo landing sties, it would be better credibility to the people who think we never got there, because they wouldn't accuse the Chinese of covering it up. The whole thing is so silly, I mean to spend a lot of money... if the moon were really that interesting, we'd be sending rovers to the moon, and we haven't sent anything there since the Apollo flights. It will bore an entire generation of rocket scientists, some of them just out of school, instead of giving them a sense of excitement that they need to have in discovery, adventure, and exploration.

Is "SpaceShip Two" part of that answer?

"SpaceShip Two" is something different. What it will do that has not been done is give a wonderful view and a feeling of weightlessness to literally hundreds of thousands of people in ten years. We're planning on building forty space ships, flying twice a day, carrying as many as eleven people at a time at affordable prices. People will fly with kids, and you've got innovative and creative people flying in space, I think it will make this dream of the movie 2001 – it will make it understandable. And every kid will know relatively soon that if he wants to, he will go to orbit in his lifetime. If that happens, then everything changes in terms of kids focusing on science or engineering. Another thing too is that the sub-orbital program will be profitable for those who fly space lines. And once it is, it will rush us to the things that are important like hotels in orbit and vacations to the moon, and that is something that is doable in my lifetime. If we don't get people involved in large numbers, we're going to just see decades of this horse shit that we've seen. We *should* say no to spending 100 billion dollars on something that doesn't reach those goals.

What has been your philosophy that you live by and that has driven you?

"Always question. Never defend." This will be something that you'll see in detail if I ever write a book. All of the people who work for me are asked to be sure to always questions things, and never defend safety. By questioning it, it gives you a smooth path to improve it. If you defend it, then you don't have a smooth path to it by admitting you were wrong and quickly moving to a solution. This is the key to success here.

Who were your heroes growing up?

It's interesting. *Aviation Weekly* did a thing in 2003 – the 100th anniversary of the Wright brothers' flight – on the most influential people in the first century of aviation history. I picked 9 folks that I thought made the big differences for aerospace, and interestingly I found that they all were little kids during the renaissance of airplanes... roughly 1908 to the end of World War l, after which airplanes sprouted all over the world. So I think all of these kids then saw all these wonderful things happening, and it caused them to be courageous risk takers and set goals very high later.

You were fourteen when Sputnik went up, so don't you parallel in a way those kids that you're talking about?

I guess so. I saw the beginning of the jet age and beginning of the missile age. When I was twelve, I saw Werner von Braun on Disney television talking about how to go to Mars. And of course Mars was a fascinating place in 1955. We thought there might even be intelligent life there. I've got a college textbook on astronomy from 1952 which debates that subject. To me von Braun was like Magellan, you know, he's going to try to go somewhere where no one's been before. That's got to be a lot more exciting than the things we do nowadays. I'd like to see NASA spend its money uncovering things that could approach that kind of a goal rather than building and flying old stuff and learning nothing new.

• • •

I had one final question for Rutan; I asked him if he saw himself as an innovator. I was goading him into boasting about himself, but he never answered the question. Rutan's planes are exciting and unique, but he is a modest man, committed to his vision, not his status. To me the coolest people do great things and let others talk about them.

So the question remains, how strong are you in the face of opposition? What's the level of your training? Have you bought into "No" so much that you begin to tell yourself "No" even *before* you want to accomplish a task? Consider this statement: "My parents made me a frightened, shut-down person, shame on them. I remained that frightened, shut-down person, shame on me." It is crucial that you learn to give yourself the permission necessary to go beyond your own "No" and accomplish your goals. But it takes training. Because the truth is, no one is going to give it to you... even when you ask for it.

It's so easy to get lost in apathy. There's so much to process, deal with, delete, distort, generalize, and ignore on a daily basis just to survive that when it comes time to really stand up, we're just too damn tired.

I JUST WANT TO BE HAPPY

At thirty-five years old, Nate was being groomed by his father to take over several restaurants in a popular chain that his father owned. Nate was married for four years with no children. He made about seventy-five thousand dollars a year, lived in a nice suburb of Los Angeles, drove a late model car, was in good physical shape and had no medical or financial problems to speak of.

Nate was miserable.

He felt that he was meant for something bigger and better than what he currently had in his life and that he was drowning is a whirlpool of mediocre achievements. He wasn't sure he wanted to be married to his wife, and he was absolutely sure that working for his father was less than gratifying.

Through further disclosure, Nate told me that when he was in college he had a strong desire to pursue a career in musical theater. He has a good command of several instruments, and he really enjoyed writing lyrics and setting them to music. His father had always wanted him to take over for him after school, and so Nate felt that if he didn't grab a foothold in a new career choice before graduation, it would be his last shot at getting out of this pre-chosen path. His father, a very traditional and stubborn man, wanted nothing to do with Nate's other passions, simply dismissing them as a "phase" he was going through.

While watching a French film one day, Nate instantly fell in love with the story. He immediately was inspired to write the story as a musical. He began work on it immediately, structuring the story for the stage, and plotting out where the songs would fit. He even got so far as to write several pieces of music with lyrics that told the story perfectly. He was on his way and felt renewed in his belief that he was meant for a more creative life than running restaurants could offer.

Thrilled with his new task, Nate shared his endeavor with his best friend, Jerry, over lunch one day. He told Jerry about the film, and how he had already structured the piece to work as a live musical in just a matter of days. His friend quickly and nonchalantly dismissed the idea, saying simply "Oh, you'll never get the rights for that movie."

In that moment, Nate's dream was dead.

Without giving one more ounce of thought or effort toward the project, Nate simply stopped without even checking to see if what his friend said was true or not.

As far as Nate was concerned, the film adaptation was his last shot at freedom from a life he was pushed into. He graduated college and immediately went to work for his father's restaurant chain, never to write another piece of music again.

By the time Nate came to see me, he was four years into his marriage, living a life of quiet desperation and resentment. He hated his father for pushing him into the restaurant business, and he resented his wife for supporting that decision.

"So what do you want?" I asked him.

"I don't know, I just want to be happy," he answered, echoing just about everyone I've ever worked with. But the key to Nate's happiness didn't lie with what he gave up, and that's what was confusing him.

Nate was furious with his friend Jerry for telling him he'd never get the rights to the movie. He was furious with his parents for pushing him into a non-creative, "dead-end" career. And he was resentful of his wife for not acknowledging his creative side.

The only person he wasn't mad at was himself! When I told him that, he was floored.

"Why should I be mad at myself?" he asked indignantly, "I didn't ask for this, it was my dad..." that's when I stopped him. Nate was blaming everyone else for him not taking risks and believing in himself when all along it was Nate who was in control of his own destiny. It was homework time.

The purpose of giving clients tasks is to shake them out of strongly-held beliefs that give them their reasons for anger and inabilities. The tougher the task, the more enlightening the discoveries, should the person choose to accept the new reality.

Nate's homework was to first interview those who he felt had pushed him into his current situation: his parents. He was reluctant to do so, stating that he would never get from them what he wanted: an apology. We shelved that idea for the moment. Instead, I instructed him to contact his friend Jerry and ask him about that moment at lunch. Again, Nate refused, saying that Jerry wouldn't remember the moment and he didn't want to start a fight with him. "A fight?" I asked, surprised that Nate felt it would escalate to an argument. "He's a friend, and I don't want to mess that up," he answered. So we moved on to his wife. I told him that he would have to sit down and talk about the choices he made and ask her to give her thoughts about it. He resisted that too.

So I handed his check back and told him we couldn't go any further.

He was surprised, to say the least. He kept asking me why. I told him simply that if he wasn't going to do the tasks I gave him – the very thing he was paying me for – that our work was done, and it would be best to part company. It was in that moment I saw a different Nate. He became apologetic, vulnerable, and had a new interest in working together.

His interviews with his father, his friend, and his wife were difficult because they required him to listen to what they were telling him. Nate had built such a story for so long that he had no control over his life and destiny, that finding out the truth – that he had the control – would mean giving up that story and taking on a new way of being. But it was the new way of being that confused him. If he couldn't blame his friends and family for not achieving his destiny, then how would blaming himself help? And what would be the result?

After Nate completed his tasks he came back to see me even more distressed than before. I have to admit I was a bit surprised. Usually after such a taxing effort, most clients feel relieved to get a new story... it can be liberating. Not with Nate. He told me that the interviews went great: his father told him that he would be happy with anything Nate did, as long as he was happy and successful. Jerry told him that he didn't remember the lunchtime conversation they had, but that no one should ever listen to him because he doesn't know anything about copyrights or how to acquire them. And his wife echoed his father's sentiments – she only wanted to see Nate happy.

So what was the issue? Nate said that while he was glad to hear that his family supported him no matter what, he was still confused about what he should do about it. Should he quit the restaurant business and take on writing again at age thirty-five? Could this be his moment?

Nate and I had to have a discussion first about why it was that he bought into the paths he thought his friends and family pushed him toward. It took a while since Nate really didn't want to see his own truth, but he finally discovered for himself that it was he – not everyone else – who didn't believe in his abilities as a musical artist. The question of his destiny as a musician was deep in his unconscious, so that when the slightest block came along, he could use that as evidence against those who loved him. The blame was conveniently placed elsewhere, and he could resign himself to a life of self-described mediocrity, all the while never taking responsibility for his own paralysis.

This was huge for Nate, not just as a realization, but also because he really had to decide for the first time on his own what he was going to do with this information.

To his credit, Nate realized that he was lucky to have an opportunity to work within a successful family business. By not having to struggle in a fickle and difficult business like musical theater, he could have the means to comfortably and securely raise a family. He was able to accept his role as husband and someday father with joy, and was grateful to let go of the anger and blame that kept him distant from the ones he loved.

As a bonus, I told Nate that giving up music entirely was a mistake. My last assignment for him was to rediscover his passion and make it a hobby. By learning to accept and love his choice of career, and finding joy through his talent on the side, Nate was complete for the first time in his life.

As a final note, it's important to see here that Nate didn't have to abandon the choices he made in life at thirty-five to pursue a career in music to be happy. He was able to see that it was *he* that said "No" to himself, and that his happiness could be found in letting go of blame, instead of taking on a career that would be inappropriate given his circumstances. Nate told me recently that he and his wife are expecting a baby, and he's never been happier.

CHAPTER FOUR HOMEWORK

Identify a time in your life when someone told you "No" and you bought into it. How is your life different because of buying in to that?

_____

_____

_____

_____

_____

_____

Write down as many passions as you can think of that you gave up on when someone or you told you no.

_____

_____

_____

_____

_____

_____

Identify three areas in your life where you tell yourself "No" on a consistent basis, such as "I'll never be thin," "I'll never find the love of my life," "I'll never make partner," "I'm too old, too fat, too slow, too tired, too young, too scared," etc.

1. _____

2. _____

3. _____

Pick the top "No" you tell yourself, and think of a person you know or are aware of that is doing the very thing you say you can't do. Make a personal study of this individual. Chances are there will be one person who personifies all of the qualities you would like to have. If you know them, you might want to interview them. If not, simply observe what it is about them that allows them to succeed where you are convinced you cannot or will not.

_____

_____

_____

_____

_____

Below, list your top ten attributes on the left side of the page. (Great personality, good sense of humor, loaded with integrity, good to animals, etc.) On the opposite side, pick the person you admire the most and list their top ten attributes. Circle all the ones you have in common. Notice how many, if any you have in common, and then take note of the different things about you. What is missing from your profile – if anything – which defines the other person's character, profile, etc, that would like to have?

YOU   THEM

_____   _____

_____   _____

_____   _____

_____   _____

_____   _____

_____   _____

_____   _____

_____   _____

_____   _____

_____   _____

Next, make a list of only the attributes that you have in common with the other person. On the other side, list the attributes you wish to have that were missing from your profile, but which you listed on his/her profile.

YOUR ATTRIBUTES   MISSING ATTRIBUTES

_____   _____

_____   _____

_____   _____

_____   _____

_____   _____

_____   _____

This will be your new "Identity Page." From now on, you will "Model" yourself, your behavior, your attitude and your actions in the same vein as your role model. By adopting the same type of thinking, you now have access to a new way of being that was not possible before. Can you see it?

Now take the work you did on the last chapter's worksheet and revise it. Simply write one sentence for each of the following questions:

"Who am I?" _____

_____

_____

"What do I want?" _____

_____

_____

"Who am I not?" _____

_____

_____

"What don't I want? _____

_____

_____

CHAPTER FIVE

ENOUGH TALK, LET'S SOLVE THIS PROBLEM!

So far in this book we've talked about finding your purpose, and we've been exploring the courage it takes to give yourself the permission to know yourself and your talents. My personal motto is "Know yourself, don't NO yourself," and even though I am an avid fan of space exploration, I still believe that the true final frontier is the vast, mysterious universe known as the human brain.

When a client comes to see me, more times that not they will ask me "Why can't I seem to have what I want?"

It's a good question, but perhaps the better way to ask it would be "What is it that I don't see about myself that is keeping me from having what I want – and furthermore why do I want it?"

In order to have true change in our lives, to create the lives that we were truly meant to live, we must first get out of our own way. We'll ask the question, "Why can't I seem to have what I want," place blame on something or someone else, let ourselves off the hook, find some comfort or attention in being a victim, and then start the cycle over again.

It's rare to find someone who is as courageously open to knowing himself as my next interview: a man who endured unimaginable pain and trauma and had the courage to ask himself how he may have been responsible for it.

ARON RALSTON

Perhaps you have seen Danny Boyle's *127 Hours*, or read Ralston's best-selling book aptly named *Between a Rock and a Hard Place*, or perhaps you heard his story on television, that unbelievable and harrowing tale of the hiker in the canyon lands of Utah who suddenly found himself trapped in a narrow sliver of rock with a half-ton boulder pinning his right hand and forearm to a sheer wall. Out of water, out of food, unable to summon help—Aron did something you could only imagine in fiction: All alone, he severed his right arm with a folding knife, and he escaped. During his captivity – five days and nights – Ralston was preparing himself emotionally for death, carving his name, date of birth and presumed date of death into the boulder, drinking his own urine because of lack of water, and videotaping his last goodbyes to his family. A note to remember: After Ralston freed himself from the boulder, he had to rappel down a 65-foot sheer wall, then hike out of the canyon in the hot midday sun.

A Phi Beta Kappa graduate from Carnegie Mellon University and an athlete, Ralston left his job as a mechanical engineer with Intel in 2002 to climb all of Colorado's "Fourteeners" over 14,000 feet high during the winter season. While he was on a canyoneering trip in Blue John Canyon (near Moab, Utah), a boulder fell and pinned his right forearm, crushing it. After Ralston was rescued, his arm was retrieved by park authorities and removed from under the boulder. It was cremated and given to Ralston. He returned to the boulder and left the ashes there. The incident has given Ralston something of a folk-hero status leading to many public appearances including the "Man-Law" series of commercials with Burt Reynolds and a burgeoning public speaking career.

Like everyone, I was fixated by Aron's story. I remember the first time I heard it in detail, watching *Dateline NBC*, and cringing at the idea of him breaking his own bones, and the sheer will and strength it took to set himself free. I shudder now at the writing of this paragraph just imagining the horror he went through.

I wanted to include his story and interview in this book not only because of the inspiration I felt hearing his thought processes as he finally summoned the courage to cut off his arm, but in the amazing and very unexpected admission he made about getting himself into the whole mess in the first place.

I met Aron about a year and a half after his incident. Despite his apparent shyness and reserved mannerisms, he is very engaging – I was impressed by his style, confidence, and the way he connects with you when he speaks to you, as if you are the only person in the room. In our interview, I wanted to get inside Aron's mind and see how much of the experience I could absorb. I knew he had been asked the same questions over and over, but something about him told me that he didn't mind at all, and that maybe this time if I asked the right question, he'd give me a whole new answer. I was right.

You survived for five days—isn't that right.

Five and a half. Five nights and on the sixth day was when I got help.

And you said you should have been dead by day four?

Certainly well before getting to the point where I actually had the opportunity to get myself free.

Right. So you were dehydrated. You had no energy and yet you not only survived but you kept coming up with plans. You tried to rig up a pulley system to get the thing off you. You had a zillion ideas. How did you do that?

I think there's a number of levels of response to that question, some of them come from the source; the source of your motivation of how do you find the power to confront your problems. And at that level it was partly taking responsibility for the fact that I had gotten myself into this situation. I had made some big mistakes –having not told anyone where I was going when I went out there by myself –had broken a cardinal rule in that sense.

And then finding the resolve in accepting the responsibility of having created this situation –that I was going to do what I could to get through it. Now that resolve was thoroughly tested through the deprivations that I endured, from dehydration, starvation, and lack of sleep.

And you were cold. Hypothermia was setting in.

Hypothermia, infection, the psychological oppression of being alone in the middle of the desert at night thinking about flash floods perhaps coming.

Did you think about maybe just ending it all?

I had to resolve foremost that *I was not going to kill myself.*

I dealt with the depression of knowing I was going to die in this canyon—that none of these options as thorough as I was to come up with them—would work. And it was then knowing that I was going to expire in this place alone why not shorten it? Why go through all that unnecessary pain if it is only going to lead to the ultimate demise?

So how did you pass the time? How did you get through it?

Some of it came from my family. It was in thinking about them. I had a video camera with me that I had pulled out from time to time –held up in front of me– and put it on the rock that was trapping my hand, and I spoke to them. First I recorded my goodbyes, my apologies. But then I turned towards the memories and recounting them as though this was going to be the videotape that was played at my funeral. I told each and every one of them how much I appreciated their presence in my life. It made me smile there despite all that I was suffering. I found a meaning to my life that made me grateful for all the experiences I'd had. Maybe that was it and it was going to be over, but those kinds of sources and resolve and determination, too. I think that's the root of the perseverance that it takes to just dedicate yourself, or for me at least, to dedicate myself to seeing it through.

Then there was the logistics how to go about actually surviving. That came from experimentation, brainstorming, things that as a mechanical engineer in a former life that I was well versed in, having been in mountain rescue knowing what it would take from hundreds of expeditions that I had undertaken—knowing what it would take to get through the moments, and as I think it was just taking it minute by minute, breath by breath, hour by hour and breaking it down in the little bits. So in those senses then finally as much as I had been controlling the experience, that I had to let go. There was a critical crossover point in letting go of understanding that you know at this point, 5 days into this, it no longer matters whether I drink my own urine or stop drinking my own urine in order to survive. It was no longer a question of really anything I could do or didn't do that was going to change the outcome of this. And for the first time, really the first time in my life, faith took a different form for me.

How so?

As opposed to an intellectual concept of letting go of that which we can't control. I actually felt an understanding that it was out of my hands quite literally. That gave me a sense of peace that carried me through until my decision to cut myself free.

Everyday you had just a sliver of sunlight, and you had a little sky, and you looked up for a sign and asked yourself-"What am I looking for? Am I looking for God to write a sign in the sky?"

And thinking "well what am I here for? This has happened for me for a reason." I'm the optimist who believes that no matter what adversity we are given it becomes a gift to us, and we just have to look for it and maybe in finding the answer to my life's purpose maybe that would just magically split the boulder in two and let me go. And now I know what I'm supposed to do with my life. There were many times that I looked for that sign that I prayed for the answer—what am I supposed to be doing, what am I supposed to be learning, what am I supposed to do here? And I've been back there even two and a half weeks ago I was back there by myself for a visit to the place. It's a deeply intense experience for me to go back and I go back pilgrimage-style to experience that. I still go through other kinds of intense challenges in my life. I stood there crying just two and a half weeks ago asking God what am I supposed to be doing with my life? And I think God came very directly into my life on the sixth morning when I was there.

In what way?

Over the days I had been trapped, I made several attempts to try to amputate my arm using this pathetically dull cheap pocketknife. But then I finally heard a voice that shouted at me with the answer that I wouldn't have to try to cut through my bones with this knife but actually that I could use the leverage of the boulder and how it had me trapped there to break the bones and then use the knife to cut through the soft tissues. It was the eureka moment, the light-bulb going off in my head. I think it was Divine interaction. Now, the bigger perspective on that is that it meant I was going to get out of there and because of that as I went through what I went through in the next hour and four minutes that I actually looked at my watch before I broke the first bone and then this smile grew on my face and I broke the second bone and that smile got bigger. And as I went through what I went through in the next hour and four minutes, I was smiling. And I think to understand that smile -- that is part of the bigger picture. It is about being motivated.

You seem like a deep person. Do you believe that you got caught in that slot for a reason?

I do. I had an out of body experience that I saw myself leaving the canyon walking through a panel that slid and opened to reveal behind this sandstone a hallway that I watched myself walk down. I don't know if you have ever seen yourself in a dream, but it is as though for me in this instance I had eyes watching me but from behind my head, watching my body walk down this hallway and then enter a living room. And there was a small child—a little boy about three years old. I saw the sliding glass door. I saw the sunshine coming through. He was playing with a truck. He had a red polo shirt on with a little insignia over the pocket. He had sensed me enter this room and I paused. He came running over to me, and I watched myself bend down and scoop him up with my left hand and I saw a handless right arm put him on my shoulder and bounce him around. This vision that out but not before I recognized a look in his eyes that said, "I'm glad you're here. Can we play now? It's great to see you." And that came for me at a pivotal time when I knew I was going to die any minute at that point. I had already etched my epitaph into the canyon wall above my shoulder. I had said my final goodbyes. And the vision of that little boy told me that if I was to see him and potentially that he was my future son, I was going to get out of that canyon. And that gave me the ability to make it through the last of those five nights when the temperature got down to thirty-five degrees and I was in shorts and a t-shirt. The hypothermia alone was costing me about six pounds of body mass per day. I was down to about 120 pounds by then.

And so your future son was – for you – the reason you believe you got into this situation?

That, and something else: I had gone out there looking for something and I don't mean just that trip, but like everything I've ever done in the outdoors has been looking for the answer to this question, "who am I?" What would I do if I was to find myself in a survival situation and in looking for those questions, I created this situation. And not only that but I had trained myself for it. I was at the peak of my physical fitness. I had all the survival training of having been on hundreds of expeditions of having undertaken an ambitious project in the mountains in the wintertime. It was all this.

Are you telling me that you were looking for this to happen?

Yes. I think I was. Not being trapped by a rock and cutting my arm off, specifically, but yes... I was out there breaking the rules. You don't hike alone, but I did. You bring a phone, but I didn't. And why? For what? I believe there was a part of me that needed to know exactly how much adversity I could handle. Honestly, I'm grateful for the experience.

Seems like a lot to me.

Yeah, but the weird thing is a year and a half ago I lost three friends to suicide, all within the span of two weeks. None of them knew each other, and yet even that experience was a gift to me. To be able to not only cherish their memories but also to use that to align my life to serve others more deeply. I am just so convinced that it was all a gift and a blessing. And most tangibly the purpose was to be able to turn me from being an inwardly-focused, pleasure seeking person to being an other-focused, serving person.

And you are now working with the disabled among others, aren't you?

I keep myself very engaged with groups ranging from at-risk youth programs and teaching climbing to young kids who've had atrocious backgrounds and yet those too become gifts for them. I work with disabled athletes, helping them to empower themselves. I work with disabled veterans who've come back from Iraq and Afghanistan missing limbs—arms and hands and just seeing —helping them experience something that puts a smile on their face. I see my ability to help others as a gift.

• • •

Aron Ralston remains one of my most memorable interviews, not just because of the severity of his injury or the dramatic tale of courage, but because of his amazing ability to step outside of himself and boldly look back in, admitting with prescient humility that there was a part of himself that needed to have – and in fact unconsciously sought out – the experience in Utah in order to find out who he really is in life and in crisis. And to take that uncommon self-awareness and turn it into a message to help others impresses me more than most people I have encountered in my life. I must admit that to this day, I remain awed by him.

I have included his story to remind you that no matter what happens in your life, and no matter what story you may tell about those experiences, you always have the opportunity to learn from, grow, and share your growth – ultimately inspiring others in the process.

Below you may see yourself in the examples and stories, but remember... there's always another way to look at it.

The Have-Do-Be Scenario

So... the race. The starting line. Remember? There you are at the starting line waiting for the gun to go off. But we already know that the runners – you included – the officials and the guy with the gun are all facets of you.

Now imagine the man with the gun never pulls the trigger.

Isn't that where you feel you are right now? Anxious, full of desire, just waiting for the gun to go off so you can get to that finish line you've been dreaming about?

You still don't have what you want. Why?

You may have spent your life working hard toward the goals that you set early on, only to find that they still lay sadly out of reach. Perhaps it's that elusive love relationship, that career, or just happiness that has never landed on your doorstep.

To get started, let's get down to the bottom of how you may have been talking to yourself. This might sound a little familiar:

"If I only had _____, then I could do _____ and finally be _____."

You can fill in the blanks with your situation. Here are a few common themes:

If I only had more money, I could buy all the things I've always wanted and never worry about my future.

If I only had that awesome car, then I could drive around showing it off and ultimately be cool!

If I only had that man, then I could get married and ultimately be happy.

If I only had that investment job, then I could do the kind of work I've always wanted and be a major player.

All great scenarios, don't you agree? And it seems logical. All we need in life is the opportunity, then we can do the thing we want and be the thing we desire to be. Happy.

But that scenario – the one that you've been living in forever – is a trap. It's actually been working against you.

I'm willing to bet that you remain unsatisfied in some area of your life; otherwise, this book would never have found its way into your hands.

So what do we do about it? First, we have to recognize the destructive nature of the "Have-Do-Be" conversation and get rid of it.

For the Chapter Four homework, I had you write down a moment in your life where you might have denied yourself of a wonderful moment, or feeling. You may have found a moment like that, but perhaps you were unable to understand why you did it. There could be many reasons, but the one that this book is focusing on – really the one I think is at the heart of most of these situations – is the phenomenon of the "Have-Do-Be" scenario.

Want to try something else? Something new?

THE CURE FOR THE HAVE-DO-BE SCENARIO

The sentence is "If I only had _____, then I could do _____ and finally be _____." That scenario truly is a 'sentence'... a life sentence that you are serving. So now you've written down your sentence(s) and you're ready to find out why the same thing you've been saying for years, the same thing you've been working for isn't actually working out, right? It's time to find out.

Imagine actually having everything you really want without ever having wanted it. Imagine 'being' happy before you have any proof that says so.

The only way to accomplish that task is to reverse the 'Have-Do-Be' scenario and take on the 'Be-Do-Have' scenario.

Be. Do. Have.

As I've mentioned, part of my experience in coaching includes training people who want to be television hosts. The number one obstacle that every single person that I worked with had believed the following:

"If I only got the hosting job, then I could do the work, see it on TV, and finally be a host!" I'm sure the thinking for actors, teachers, doctors, lawyers, construction workers, and just about everyone else isn't too dissimilar.

So the students came to me hoping I could give them the short cut, or the magic pill to help them get the job that will validate their life choice. In essence, they didn't believe they were hosts yet. So how was anyone supposed to hire them? That would be like a doctor saying, "If I could just get a chance to cut into a patient, I would finally be a surgeon." Well, obviously doctors and TV hosts have different challenges before them to achieve their goal, but what the average hosting student doesn't realize is everything they need to be a host – all the training, all the knowledge – is already within them, they're just waiting for someone else to give the permission to unlock it.

Sticking with the talent scenario, imagine a casting office. In it sit a producer, a camera and sound operator, and the casting associate who is responsible for bringing in a variety of people to be seen for the role of "host" of the show.

Let's just say the show by the way is a travel show. They're looking for someone to go from town to town and uncover all the strange oddities that make up that particular area. This fictional show is called *Unique Spots: America.*

The producers hire the casting director to bring in good candidates for the show – someone who can carry it without stealing it, the one who can bring out the best in the town, and get the most of the people they interview. Bright, confident and in charge... That's all they want. So the casting director picks ten candidates and after that it's up to the producers to make their choice.

Of those ten choices let's say nine of them (and this is pretty typical) are thinking, "I wonder what they want? Do they want me to be funny? Mysterious? Who do they want me to be?"

Are you getting the point here?

The tenth candidate knows the truth of the situation and will most times book the show simply because of that knowledge. The truth of the matter is the producers don't know what they want! They're just hoping someone will come in and show them. They know one thing: They want the person to be confident.

When those other nine candidates enter the room, the first thing they display is fear. The next thing is something I call the "kill me" expression. It's hard to describe other than it comes from the position of "I'm a little lamb and when you want to you can attack and kill me, so I'm going to keep my head down and show you fear." I know, it's a little dramatic, but I told you it was hard to describe!

This form of posturing, or lack thereof, is death to an auditioner. Think of it in terms of a blind date: You're both meeting for the first time, if one of you is scared and hoping the other one likes you, it puts the pressure on the other one to do so, and most likely they won't.

But the one that walks in that room with the attitude of "What's up... this is me, dig it?" is the one that's going to take the pressure off the chooser and make the choice easy. That's the one who will get the job.

That tenth person wasn't waiting for the job to tell them who they are... they simply were the host long before they walked into that room. That's an example of the "Be-Do-Have" scenario: He was the host, walked in and DID the job without reservation, and GOT the show as a result.

By the way... all of my former students were instructed using the "Be-Do-Have" model, and many of them are working television personalities today. I'm very proud of them all!

So... who do you want to BE, but are waiting for someone else to give you the permission to be it?

DEATH DOESN'T BECOME HER

Carol was an NLP client of mine in the summer of 2005. She came to me because she was really unhappy but didn't know why. All she knew was that she wanted to be happier.

Through the course of getting her detailed personal history, I was able to uncover that this 35-year-old, married, mother of two workaholic simply never gave time to herself for anything. It was job, husband and kids 24/7, and she simply didn't make time to do what she wanted. Notice I didn't say "have the time."

Her life was all about taking care of everyone. In the morning she got the kids up, made sure they were dressed and ready for school, got their lunches made, fixed breakfast for her husband who had to be at work by 6am, took the kids to the bus, dropped her husband off at work, and continued to her own job at a bank. At the bank she was a project manager. She was in charge of making sure that each person below her was on track with details and deadlines. She reported to her superior who also benefited from Carol's help with his responsibilities as well. In the evening, Carol picked up the kids from school, make their dinners, got them to bed, cleaned up the house and maybe had time to talk with her husband, or call or email friends before exhaustion took over. She was at the point where she felt trapped. She didn't like the toll her schedule was taking on her, but she knew that no one else could do everything that she was doing as well.

Added to that was her growing resentment of her husband for not stepping up and doing more for the family financially and physically.

As time went on, I found out that when she was a young girl – maybe seven years old – Carol's close family member died at the age of forty. Carol assumed at that point that she would never make it past forty, and her job in that case was to make sure that everyone was taken care of while she was around. I was surprised to hear that she absolutely was convinced that she wouldn't make it past 40, and because of that she didn't just turn into a drug addict or a vegetable. Instead she did the opposite. She became the hero.

So you might say that Carol at an early age told herself NO. "No, I'm not going to live past forty years old," and so she turned it into a positive by taking care of her husband and kids to make sure they were going to be okay. That's a good thing, right?

Of course not!

The only way Carol could prove that she was going to die at forty was if she planned to kill herself! And she might have been doing that through stress... remember Mel Chang? But by deciding she was going to die at forty, Carol did neglect one very important detail in her life: Herself. She said "No" to her own possibilities by buying into a decision made by a seven-year-old!

The first thing we had to do was get it out of her head that she was automatically destined for the grave in five years. This was a tougher thing to do than it might sound. Carol spent most of her life with this agenda in mind and had built a life around it. To change course required an in depth look at the cost of her behavior.

First, her resentment. By taking over all the duties at home and office, Carol was certainly fulfilling her role as doomed caretaker, but the people around her were missing out on her greatness. Carol never laughed. She never went to lunch with coworkers. She never made a space for others to be light-hearted or teasing with her. And most importantly, she resented her husband for not doing the things that she never even allowed him to do. Totally unaware that she had cornered the market in responsibility; she simply thought that no one else needed or wanted to handle the things she was taking on.

By looking at the rift she was creating in her marriage – an obvious and unconscious emotional separation to prepare him for her death – she was able to see how much hurt – not help – she was bringing to her home. By looking at her obsessive need for control at work, doing the jobs of her subordinates as well as her superior, she was alienating those who wanted to prove themselves and move up, and creating an atmosphere of codependence with her boss. There was no freedom anywhere in her life anywhere.

Carol was able to see that she wasn't helping others to get on without her, she was shutting them out of their own relationships with their potential, and with her. Her "No" became everyone else's "No." Do you know anyone like that? How do you feel when you're around them... more or less free to be yourself? Or is this you I'm talking about. If so, how do you think others feel if you're always in control?

The next step for Carol was to get her started on a ten-year plan (pushing past her designated death age by five years,) designed to allow her to find herself for the first time.

When she first came to see me, she brought a very colorfully decorated notebook. I immediately noticed it and asked her if she decorated it. She did. Throughout the course of our meetings, I noticed more and more that she had very artistic tendencies. When I finally asked her to tell me more about it, she opened up like I'd never seen her do. She went on and on about how she would love to teach art, or do scrapbooking as a hobby, or open an art supplies and coffee shop. She stopped short of telling me that she would never do that because she thought she would be dead by forty, but I knew why.

This was the ticket to her freedom and the freedom of everyone around her. I told her to dedicate a portion of each Friday to setting up her guest room as a part-time scrapbooking room. "I can't do that," she complained, "I have to pick up the kids and make them dinner!" I had her go to her husband and tell him this. He immediately offered to take over, telling her that she never allowed him the chance to pick up the kids and he would love to! She began to question her resentment of him.

Once the scrapbooking was under way, I had her investigate other areas in her life where she could express herself artistically. She did some research and found a couple adult classes in her area – also on Fridays – and she signed up immediately.

We came to call Fridays "Freedom Friday," a very important day for her to find her new life through self expression and letting go of controlling her family and coworkers.

In a strange twist of fate, the company she worked for fell victim to the recession. As of this edition, Carol is three years into her ten-year plan. And because of her self-motivation, she is far along into creating the artist's studio/coffee shop she always dreamed of having, but until recently never gave herself permission to make a reality. Just think about where she would be now if she never took action on her dreams.

Death is the reason we fear everything. Death is the reason I wrote this book. Death is the inevitable and silent puppet master controlling virtually every choice and decision we make from top to bottom. Death is coming and there's absolutely nothing we can do about it. Nothing. And when there's nothing there, then everything is possible. Everything.

In his magnificent book *The End of Faith*, Sam Harris makes the following point:

We are terrified of our creaturely insignificance, and much of what we do with our lives is a rather transparent attempt to keep this fear at bay.

Carol, a rare case, actually was preparing for her death. In the process of doing so, she forgot to live. I agree with Harris and think most of us – if not all of us to a certain extent – unconsciously see death as something we might actually be able to avoid somehow if we only ignore it, or strongly subscribe to the notion of the afterlife. But in the process of ignoring the inevitable, we still make it real by making it something to ignore or slough off, and therefore our denial of death simply puts us in a state of unconscious fear. The wonder of life and what truly is the best part of living, learning, growth and connectedness, is what makes life worth living now.

You want to leave a legacy? You want to live beyond your own life? Good. Me too. The last thing you should do is forget to manage your well being now.

CHAPTER FIVE HOMEWORK

First, write down your own sentence, filling in the structure below. If you've got more than one, write them all down. Be as honest with yourself as possible, and don't think about what you're writing, or how you can respond perfectly; just simply write what you feel. Hang on to those sentences; we'll review them later.

If I only had _____

Then I'd do _____

And finally be _____

Now, Take those examples and reverse them using the "Be-Do-Have" scenario. Example: "I'm happy and accepted. I'm going to treat myself with acceptance, and speak to others without judgment. I will thus have acceptance."

I can be (I am) _____

Therefore I will _____

And have _____

Hang on to those sentences. Put them up on your wall or your bathroom mirror to look at every day. Remember... this is your training.

CHAPTER SIX
WOMEN MAKING A DIFFERENCE

A CONFERENCE OF THEIR OWN

For the last three years, I have been fortunate enough to have been asked by Sirius Satellite Radio to attend the California Governor's and First Lady's Conference on Women. Each year Maria Shriver opens the doors at the Long Beach Convention Center in California to over 20,000 attendees (mostly women) who spend the day hearing stories of amazing women who – against all odds – fought for their place in the world and in history.

For the 49% of us who have no idea what it's like to be a woman, spending one day at this conference will give you a pretty good idea. After three years of attendance, I can honestly say that I'm at least a little closer to understanding the fair sex.

I began writing this book around the same time I was attending these conferences, and I quickly realized there was so much for these women to say about the struggle of not taking no for an answer and fighting not only the status quo, but whatever biases existed against them because of their gender.

MARIA SHRIVER

My first goal for this chapter was to interview Maria Shriver, then still the first lady of California, still the wife of Governor Arnold Schwarzenegger, NBC reporter, niece to John, Bobby and Ted Kennedy, daughter of Eunice Kennedy Shriver, philanthropist, mother, activist, and soul searcher.

During the first two years I attended the conference, I simply watched Maria preside over the events she created with magnificent grace. I saw a growing movement, which – until Maria took it over – was a small gathering of a few women. I saw famous and important women such as Michelle Obama, Sarah Ferguson, Gloria Steinem, Sally Ride, Madeleine Albright and so many others speak to thousands of women. I saw leaders and icons such as the Dali Lama, Bono, and Tony Blair speak as well. I met and spoke with scores of women who had taken time off from work or family responsibilities – some traveling across the country – to attend. By my third year, I awed at the spectacle Maria had cooked up: Sirius Radio and television coverage; standing-room-only attendance – over 20,000 women; and a live appearance by the governor, Arnold Schwarzenegger himself. (I was determined to get that interview as well! More on that later.)

After three consecutive years of spending time at the conference, I felt as though I had come to know Maria. She holds nothing back. She shares all of herself: fears; flaws; and fortunately, she is an open book, and one worth reading.

Being Maria Shriver, I found out, is no easy task. It's walking a line between journalist and politician. Between being a mother and a daughter, a woman and a leader, a niece and a cousin and an aunt, and most of all a seeker. To come to know Maria as I have over the years is to know a truly whole and complete woman who wears her flaws and struggles on her sleeve as much as she wears her family's honorable pride and history. She is a courageous person who reminds the women who attend her conference each year – and ultimately all of us – that true strength comes not from ignoring your weaknesses, but embracing them. Happiness is not a destination, but a daily choice. She told the gatherers at this year's conference the following:

"I have learned that the reason hat we're here is to love one another, to connect with one another... to truly see one another... we're here, I believe, to experience moments of fear and pain and joy and I've learned that all of those feelings are okay. I have learned that at the age of fifty-two that listening is love. And I've learned this too: If you allow yourself to be broken open, that underneath that is who you are. I know it's so hard and so scary to let the real you unfurl, and getting there takes time... Feeling afraid isn't weakness, it's the beginning of strength."

As I looked around the room while Maria was speaking, I experienced the silent awe from her listeners. This wasn't the first time either. I saw it the year before and the year before that. And it's not Maria's power that levels people, it's her humility. It's her honesty and her openness.

Most of this book was written in late 2009, but several additions have been made recently to reflect the changing times. One such change is the relationship between Arnold Schwarzenegger and Maria Shriver. As of this edition in mid-2011, they are going through what appears to be the initial stages of a divorce. At the time I interviewed Maria none of this scandal had broken. Later on in the book I will make references to Arnold Schwarzenegger and my attempts to interview him – also written before the scandal. My opinion of the infidelity and the break up of their marriage is not important. What is important is that I know Maria will take this mess and turn it into her message. She'll take this test and make it her testimony. That is who she is.

I had just a few moments with Maria this year – as I did with each woman I interviewed – and with that time she was able to impart to me her philosophy of not taking "No" for an answer:

What is your philosophy for not taking "No" for an answer, and where did you learn it?

Well, I learned not to take No for an answer from my mother, who works on behalf of people with intellectual disabilities and everything she wanted to start for people with intellectual disabilities, she was told No. Do not take people out of institutions; people with intellectual disabilities cannot compete on the playing field…No, No, No. But she just kept going and kept going. And in my journalism, I was told No almost daily. No, you can't book this person, No you can't have that shot, No you can't do this. I just have found ways to come around the other side and that's really helped me in my work here as first lady because people say no to you a lot. No, you can't do that. What do you think; you're going to have a million women on the web? What do you mean, you want to make this the biggest women's forum. No, no, first ladies don't do that, they don't act that way, they don't speak out like that. No. And I think that it's important to learn how to say no yourself to protect your time and your boundaries, but I think it's important to understand that "No" is just a word.

How has your philosophy served you in creating this conference for women?

Really by expanding what I started five years ago: I

wanted to ad a night before event, so I came up with the concept of the village, a mall for your mind, body and spirit. I wanted to give women the chance to meet authors, to hear other speakers, and be with one another, meeting other entrepreneurs and do business with them. And I think all of that has occurred beyond my wildest expectations. This conference sells out quickly now, so I wanted to get a million women on the web to watch this conference. We're at the women's history museum in Seneca Falls, New York, where the women's movement started, that was very important for me. And I wanted to keep mixing it up and surprising people. I wanted to add more men I admire who I think have a message. All of that was possible this year, and I'm thrilled with the way it's turned out.

• • •

While I would never presume to call Maria Shriver a friend, it warms me to know that each year as I return to the conference, she looks to me with fond recognition, and it's always a nice reunion. She is perhaps the most amazing and complete woman I know, and the coolest thing about her is that she's the last one who would agree. And despite her experience with the end of her marriage, I know that Maria Shriver will turn that mess in to a powerful message. That's just who she is.

The second year Maria ran the conference, it was titled "Architects of Change." Many great speakers graced the stage, but one lit it up and that person was Suze Orman. She told her amazing story to the 20,000 person crowd, some of which I will share with you below, along with our very brief interview:

SUZE ORMAN

You probably think that Suze Orman was born a financial guru and has always known how to manage money. Actually she wasn't, and hasn't. Her mother was a secretary and supported her family. You know Suze as a brilliant communicator, and probably think she has never had a problem with public speaking. Nope. When she was 6years old, she had a speech impediment, she couldn't pronounce R's, T's or S's correctly, so the word "Beautiful" came out "Boobidle." And forget trying to say the world "Restless!" She knew at an early age that she – as she puts it – "was dumb!" So she decided not to even try. All through grade school and into high school, her grades were abysmal. She says often that she's surprised she even graduated. College was no different. When she graduated, she borrowed $1,500 from her brother and lived in a van in Berkeley for three months, ultimately landing her dream job: Waitress at the age of thirty.

After seven years, several of her long-time customers at the restaurant pooled their money and gave her checks totaling $50,000 to help her start her own restaurant. The first thing she did was head down to Merrill Lynch and opened up an account. A stock broker whom she hired to manage her funds convinced her that signing blank pages that he handed her would ensure that her money would grow and she would be earning an extra $100 a week. She was more than happy to sign. Within three months all of the money was lost.

So with her money gone, she decided that in order to pay her benefactors back, she marched into Merrill Lynch – the very place that lost her money – to apply for a job. Dressed in red and white striped pants tucked into cowboy boots, she was not your average-looking stockbroker. When asked why she chose to dress in that fashion, she answered, "Well, looking around, I don't see any other women. There are no role models for me, I don't know how else to dress." But wardrobe dysfunction aside, the head manager of the branch decided to hire her, saying "You know Suze, women belong barefoot and pregnant, you'll be out of here in six months, but I need to hire you to fill our women's quota." To which Suze replied: "Alright... how much are you going to pay me to get me pregnant?"

While she was there, studying to be a stockbroker, Suze learned that what her broker did with her $50,000 was illegal. You can't invest people's money the way they did if they can't afford to lose it. When she brought it to the attention of the head manager, he told her that he makes them a lot of money and she would be best suited to sit at her desk, continue working and not say another word about it. And she did for a while, but soon she began to realize that it didn't matter how much that broker made the company, what he did was wrong. And she had to now do what was right, so she sued Merrill Lynch while she was working for them!

She immediately thought that would mean her job was over, but under whistleblower protection, she could sue them without being fired. Two years later, Merrill Lynch settled, gave her back all the money plus 18% interest, because at the time Suze had become their sixth highest producing broker.

Suze shared her story that day at the conference not to impress anyone, but to inspire everyone. As she points out, it doesn't matter if you can't speak well, it doesn't matter if you can't read well, if your grades are bad, if you live on the streets in a van, or your mother was just a secretary. As Suze so aptly pointed out: "There are no excuses big enough that you can have to keep you from being an architect of change. Change in your own life, change in the lives of others, Change! But you've got to change how you feel about yourself. You can't think less of yourself. You can't do less for yourself. And you simply have to go within to find out why you are willing to do without. Wish well for others, because an other's success will not keep you down."

When I caught up with Suze, I asked her what inspired her.

"What inspires me, and had always inspired me, are the people who don't have any money. Even though they don't have money to feed their families, light their homes with utilities, they still have smiles on their faces. It's actually discovering what you don't know that you already have that is the key. Remember that when things happen to you that you don't think are so good, they are actually a blessing in disguise if you would just look at it that way."

Of all the women interviewed, I find Suze's story to be the most entertaining. You really need to go see her speak; she'll have you not only inspired to be great, but rolling in the aisle.

She's also been an amazing resource for women during this period of recession. To think about where she came from to become one of the top financial advisors for American women is truly inspiring.

• • •

CHRISTIANE AMANPOUR

Born in London to an Iranian father and British mother, Christiane spent most of her childhood growing up in Tehran. The Amanpours led a privileged life under the government of the Shah of Iran. She returned to England in 1969, and her family fled Iran after the Islamic Revolution. She moved to the United States to study journalism at the University of Rhode Island. During her time there she worked in the News Department at WBRU-FM Providence. Amanpour graduated from URI summa cum laude with a Bachelor of Journalism degree in 1983. She was hired by CNN as a desk assistant on the Foreign Desk. In 1989, she was posted to Frankfurt, Germany, where she reported on the democratic revolutions sweeping Eastern Europe at the time.

It was her coverage of the Persian Gulf War that followed Iraq's occupation of Kuwait in 1990 that made her famous, while also taking the network to a new level of news coverage. She also reported from the Bosnian war and many other conflict zones. Her emotional delivery from Sarajevo during the siege of Sarajevo led some viewers and critics to question her professional objectivity, claiming that many of her reports were unjustified and in favor towards the Bosnian Muslims, to which she replied, "There are some situations one simply cannot be neutral about, because when you are neutral you are an accomplice. Objectivity doesn't mean treating all sides equally. It means giving each side a hearing." From 1996–2005, she was contracted by *60 Minutes*-creator Don Hewitt to file four to five in-depth, international news reports a year as a special contributor. These reports garnered a Peabody Award in 1998. Based out of CNN's London bureau, Amanpour is one of the most recognized international correspondents on American television, with a willingness to work in dangerous conflict zones. It has been said of her, "If there's war, there's Amanpour."

At the women's conference, Ms. Amanpour related her philosophy of not only serving others' needs, but in maintaining one's own integrity and self-interested throughout. I asked her about the speech. Here's what she said:

"My thoughts about my speech were simple. One has to be a citizen of this world, not just to inhabit the planet. I wanted a sort of a call to action to a new generation of Americans to go out and take their talent and success around the world and make the world like America again and restore America's reputation. And it's very important that you should know, this is not about a popularity contest, it's not just so that we're liked, it's in order to get America's vital business done. To be respected, to be admired again, to get people out there again to think that it's cool to share America's unique ideals, to respect the good name of freedom and not let that languish as a dirty word and just to get this country back on track again. And then, I was speaking up for journalism, what I believe to be true journalism, not that it's my job to set an agenda or to decide on who or what, but to ask the rigorous questions, to do the reporting and let others decide."

What is your philosophy about not taking "No" for an answer?

Well look, I've always known throughout my career that you have to believe in something. What is my job? It's about telling the truth. It's about unveiling things that others would like to keep hidden. It's about holding power accountable. It's about trying to help those who suffer injustice and oppression. So, it's not about me. And our profession is in danger. I believe we need to stand up for this profession, now more than ever. We need strong, robust, independent journalists who'll report without fear, or favor and will go out there and tell the truth.

And then she was off... to her next story, I imagine.

•   •   •

GLORIA STEINEM

You can't be a woman today and not feel something about Gloria Steinem. Steinem was born in Toledo, Ohio. Her mother, Ruth, was of part German descent. Her Jewish father, Leo Steinem, was a traveling antiques dealer. Steinem credits her mother as the central figure in her life who raised her consciousness to include the understanding of social injustices. Steinem, in what she later called her first "serious assignment," wrote a piece for *Esquire* Magazine regarding contraception. Her resulting 1962 article about the way in which women are forced to choose between a career and marriage preceded Betty Friedan's book *The Feminine Mystique* by one year.

In 1963, working on an article for Huntington Hartford's *Show* magazine, she was employed as a Playboy Bunny at the New York Playboy Club. The article featured a photo of Steinem in Bunny uniform and exposed how women were treated at the clubs. The article was a sensation, making Steinem an in-demand writer in the process. Steinem took a job at Felker's *New York* magazine in 1968. In 1972, she co-founded the feminist-themed *Ms.* magazine. It began as a special edition of *New York* magazine, and Felker funded the first issue. When the first regular issue hit the newsstands in July 1972, its 300,000 "one-shot" test copies sold out nationwide in eight days. It generated an astonishing 26,000 subscription orders and over 20,000 reader letters within weeks.

Later, working for George McGovern, Steinem became politically active in the feminist movement and in 1971; she co-founded the National Women's Political Caucus as well as the Women's Action Alliance. She has fought against pornography (versus the kinder, gentler and more equal "erotica"), female genital mutilation, the reversal of abortion rights, and the general domination of one sex or individual over another.

Some had called her the mother of the feminist movement... a movement which radically changed this country and woke up countless men and women to a new, advanced reality which many women today take for granted, to which Steinem replies "Great!"

I caught up with her at the women's conference and noticed immediately a crowd surrounding us. It was clear that of all the personalities speaking that day, Gloria Steinem was a living legend.

How important is a gathering like this... this conference?

You know, this is what movements are all about. You have to come together and understand that you're not alone. Hear other people with similar situations, otherwise we get isolated, so there's nothing more important than conferences like this and continuing them in our lives, so that we have some cell or group or book club or consciousness raising...it doesn't matter what you call it...quilting bee... something that people who support us and help us understand that the issues that are represented here are majority issues, but because we don't see them in the institutions of our country or the media as much as we should, we come to feel crazy and alone, unless we have the occasional booster shot of creating a temporary nation which is what's being created here.

I think too if we have one generation of children raised without violence, we don't know what might be possible. We have no idea because violence feels inevitable and like home, that we do it in the street and we do it in foreign policy, when we don't have to.

What do you tell young women who might take the modern feminist movement for granted?

Well, I think when we're kids, whether we're boys or girls, we say, 'It's not fair.' And then we get talked out of the idea that we can fix unfairness. Hang on to that childhood voice that says it's not fair and make sure that you get together to fix what's not fair and set higher sights. You know, I think we finally understand that women can do what men can do, but we don't yet understand that men can do what women can do. So, until men are raising little kids as much as women are, it won't work. And, also kids won't know that men are as loving and nurturing as women are.

What's your philosophy on not taking "No" for an answer?

I think probably, for most women, I don't mean to generalize, but I think women have a harder time taking Yes for an answer. Because we're so self-critical and we're so convinced we have to be perfect - instead of just the same as Irving, or whoever had the job before – that it's probably more difficult. I mean if you compliment a woman, she will tell you what's wrong with her. What helps me the most is to realize that if you're not part of the accepted group – whatever that may be – nothing you do is right. So you might as well do what you fucking well please.

• • •

After talking with Ms. Steinem, something occurred to me that I had never thought before: People are afraid of you when you stick to your guns, don't apologize for who you are, and look them in the eye while you're getting what you want. So many of us apologize for asking for – or demanding – what we want and deserve, if we fight for it at all. We get labeled "activists" or "whining liberals," but – and this is the kicker – only by the people from whom we are demanding change, and who have the most to lose as a result. It's funny... there was a part of me that was intimidated by Gloria Steinem before I met her. That part has been educated and charmed.

JENNY MCCARTHY

Most of us know Jenny McCarthy as two people: The Playboy playmate who turned TV host and *Maxim* magazine contributing columnist, media darling and movie star; and her more recent and serious identity as a mother who has a son diagnosed with autism.

The disorder of McCarthy's son, Evan, began with seizures, and his improvement occurred after the seizures were treated; these symptoms are more consistent with Landau-Bluffer syndrome, which often is misdiagnosed as autism. McCarthy served as a spokesperson for Talk About Curing Autism (TACA) from June 2007 until October 2008. She participated in fundraisers, online chats, and other activities for the non-profit organization to help families affected by autism-spectrum disorders. Her first fundraiser for TACA, Ante Up for Autism, was held on October 20, 2007, in Irvine, California. Her book on the subject, *Louder than Words: A Mother's Journey in Healing Autism* was published September 17, 2007. Her subsequent book Mother Warriors: A Nation of Parents Healing Autism Against All Odds took the case for the cure even further. She told Oprah Winfrey that her son was developing normally until he received his measles, mumps, and rubella vaccine (at fifteen months of age) and claimed that they were the cause. She has stated on many talk shows and at rallies that Chelation Therapy helped her son recover from autism; the underlying rationale for Chelation, which is that mercury in vaccines causes autism, has been roundly rejected by scientific studies, with the National Institute of Mental Health concluding that autistic children are unlikely to receive any benefit in return for the risk of cognitive and emotional problems due to the chelating agent itself. But Jenny remained resolute, after countless doctors told her that her son would not be healed, she found a way through diet and therapy to get her son back. Imagine if she had simply taken "No" for an answer.

She was at the women's conference to share her story and let her audience know that we don't have to accept the first, second, or even ninth answer we receive... there is always another answer, and even after a thousand "No's," there can be a "Yes" and that's when everything is possible.

Your story is not only one of success, but one of transformation. You're here this year as a pioneer, as a mother, and as a leader. Is that a different feeling for you?

To come now as a speaker makes me feel good only because I feel like I'm representing a huge part of the American population who have children who are sick and who are lost because of the healthcare that is not given to us. So, I do feel like I'm standing on a bunch of women's shoulders that brought me to this moment as I sit here next to you.

You knew that what you were hearing from the doctors wasn't enough for you. How? How do you not trust a trained professional?

You know, instinct is a really powerful tool. It's a very real thing, and you hear those stories about mom's feeling their child being sick from across town or something happening. You know, because we're all connected energetically, it's a very real tool and, you know, without it, I would not have gotten Evan recovered from autism. And without it, I wouldn't be doing what I am doing, which is being everyone's voice in this. I would have continued on to yuk it up on stage 19 at Paramount doing some comedy. Instead, I am breaking down doors and trying to change the old paradigm of medicine and kind of help save this generation as best I can.

Where did you summon the strength to overcome the "No's" you were facing and fight for what was in your heart/ gut?

I have always been an outspoken individual, so I knew that I had the strength and power to work as hard as I had to both for my son and then for this community of families that have been trying to be heard. I did what I had promised I would do, I got my son better and I told the world how I did it and how they can too.

I have been fortunate enough that as a celebrity, I was able to get our message heard. I am so pleased with the progress that has been made in the past three years alone, but there is still a long path ahead and so much more that needs to be done.

I just talked with Gloria Steinem. How glad are you that she came before our generation? Has it made it easier?

Yes! And you know, this is a new era of female empowerment and you can really feel it, especially coming here, that I think it's like 15,000 people coming to become empowered and make change and I think women are now realizing that we have the capability and we have a voice that can move mountains. I mean, consider what I've done in one year. People weren't talking about autism or the controversy or the things that I've been bringing up and it's all happening because I'm a mom and I have a story and has nothing to do with whether I have a penis or a vagina. But I'm happy to be part of it and hope Maria asks me back next year because I do enjoy making change.

Tell me how you learned not to take "No" for an answer?

The not taking No for an answer came from when I first moved out to Los Angeles and people told me I would never make it. So, I got the old 'No.' There's no way you can be a host, there's no way you can be an actress, there's no way you can be a model, there's no way. And I am so grateful for those No's. Because those No's really empower you to prove yourself. It's kind of like having parents that say you'll never amount to anything or your aunts and uncles think you're trash and you work so hard your whole life to prove them wrong. Not that that's necessarily the right way to go about things, but not taking No for an answer gets shit done. It just does.

Was there ever a moment where you questioned "Why me, why my son?" Did that happen, and if so, how did you fight the urge to feel sorry for yourself and conquer those feelings?

Thankfully, I do not struggle with the 'Why Me' anymore. I know that everything that has happened in my life with Evan was because I was supposed to make people aware of the issues behind this epidemic and the treatment options that are available to these families.

Why do you think so many people accept the first answer they're given in life, and what do you say to those who take no for an answer, or are afraid to confront 'conventional wisdom'?

Sometimes it can be easier for us to accept what we are told. But if there is any possibility of making our child feel better or allowing our child to live a happier life, isn't that worth all the inconvenience in the world? To go against the norm or to question authority is not something that is instilled in us, it is something that we have to be strong enough to do for those that are not able to – the children.

Why does it take a Jenny McCarthy, a Christopher Reeve, an Elizabeth Glazer, a Jerry Lewis Telethon, etc. to bring about change that should be a natural part of our evolving humanity – should already be a given, and what can we do to make our lives better now?

We all need to be more aware of what we put into our body and how it makes us feel. Question where things come from and make changes in your own life.

What has the reaction been to your cause?

The parents that are realizing that when the doctors give them a dead end sentence of; there's nothing you can do – they're not believing that anymore. I think people are starting to question authority. That's the day and age now. If you want to encompass everything that I believe in, people are questioning authority, that we are seekers of truth. We're seekers of hope and when people say no and people say it's a dead end, this generation of women are going, "I don't believe you, I'm going to keep going." And that's what I've hopefully started with moms and hope to continue for generations to come.

Share her opinion or not, Jenny McCarthy is a fighter. She fights for her son and she fights for her beliefs, just like all the other women I interviewed in this book. They are a testament to those who bypass the No's in their life and follow the Yes's.

• • •

One thing that stood out for me at the conference – hearing the speakers and talking with those amazing women – is the real sense of struggle women must still go through to be heard, to have their interests addressed, to be taken seriously, and to be counted as equals. They have come a long way it's true, but it seems that the fight is still far from over. If anyone in the world needs a mentor, a fighter, a hero, look at the women in your life.

We've spent a good amount of time talking about not taking "No" for an answer, we've progressed through the exercises designed to shake up your old ways of thinking, and we've seen some strong examples of individuals who have risen above self-doubt and opposition to achieve their goals. At this point it should be getting a little clearer to you that it's as easy to say "Yes" as it is to say "No," we're just used to taking the easy way out. "No" is very easy. It's clean and final. No one has to get hurt. "Yes" is complicated: you've got to prove your point; stay a little longer; fight for you piece of the pie; *and allow yourself to achieve the goal!*

Look at Jenny McCarthy; a beautiful model, TV host, movie star and author who had everything going for her, until she was blind-sided by her son's autism. Did she ignore the problem and live her life in denial, passing him off to special caretakers to deal with him? No. Did she take the doctor's word that there was nothing that could be done? No. Instead, this wild, fun-loving, carefree celebrity became an activist for her son's challenge, raising awareness about the causes and possible treatments surrounding autism. She went on *Oprah*, wrote a book, talked to anyone who would listen. She put aside herself and her career and found an extraordinary new role as the voice of hope for parents all over the world who had given up. Now she's leading the charge for a better way of life with a new talk show and productions that have value. She made lemonade out of her lemons! (I can hear her laughing at that right now!)

THE TRAGIC CASE OF THE BEAUTIFUL FACE

I do a lot of traveling in my career, and as a result I see and meet countless people in my travels. Recently, on a trip to New York, I saw evidence of a scenario I have come to call "The Tragic Case of the Beautiful Face."

Being a talent and life coach, I have mostly worked with women, and most of them have come to me with the desire to be in a committed relationship. And a great majority of them (remember I live in L.A.) are very beautiful women.

Sitting in the terminal at J.F.K., I was waiting to board my plane when I see two young women walk by. One of them was tall, leggy, dressed perfectly, with great hair and beautiful face. She walked with such an air of confidence and she knew exactly why. She – as Dennis Miller puts it – "won the Darwinian lottery."

Her friend was not like her. Her body was a little dumpier, hair wasn't as shiny, her clothes weren't meticulously chosen, and her face wasn't a statue candidate. And her posture reflected that. Her shoulders were hunched forward a bit, and she looked down when she walked. The beautiful girl carried a *Vogue* magazine, the other girl carried books.

And all I could think was that I felt really sorry for that pretty girl. We'll get back to her later.

In 1999 when I started coaching I was amazed at how difficult it was for my more attractive female students to let go of whatever fear they had getting in front of the camera. I mean it... most of them walked in to class with head high and confidence expressed, but when it was time to walk up to the camera and simply be themselves, they just had nowhere to go. Hosting demands authenticity and the ability to be open and vulnerable. When faced with that, most beautiful women – who mostly project from the outside – are faced with a confusing dilemma when it comes to being real.

Then there's the girl who apologizes for it. I'll pick one for my example. I'll call her Cynthia.

Cynthia came to one of my classes to make the transition from fashion model to host an easy one. The first thing I noticed about her was her beauty. The next thing I noticed was her act.

Her act was to be the sweetest girl possible to everyone in the room. Certainly not an undesirable quality, but her reasons for the behavior (which I found out later were epidemic amongst women like her) were much more complex than the sweet simple nature she put forth.

Cynthia had known all her life that she was a beautiful girl. She wasn't obsessed with beauty; it was bestowed upon her and she just went with it. She modeled early and was successful. She got all the attention, all the accolades, and would no doubt get many hosting jobs in the future. But everything about her told me that she was apologetic about it.

Once she got in front of the camera, I told her that she had to shed the "act" and be herself. Hosting is no different than how you would talk with your friends at a party – it's really a no brainer – but most of my students at first think it means you have to be someone you're not, and that's why it's so hard for some people. They make the camera lens a mirror. That's a mistake.

Cynthia spent her life surrounded with admirers, agents, managers, handlers, fans and photographers. And she was very lonely. She told me one day that she never really had friends, and certainly has no girlfriends, and so she became extra sweet to everyone to make them like her more.

Like her more?

She was unconsciously convinced that no one liked her because they were jealous of her beauty, so naturally she wanted to be liked and became a very sweet, likable person. But along the way she lost who she really was, and it showed immediately on camera when all she had to do was be herself.

Cynthia became an NLP client of mine and we worked through those issues.

Imagine living in a world where, simply because of your genetic make up, you're immediately pre-judged to the point where no one gives you credit for being a real person with deep feelings, bad days, fears, doubts, concerns, desires for companionship and connection and everything else that makes us all human. Think about it... do you empathize with Cynthia, or do you think she's not allowed to have problems?

Underneath, Cynthia never allowed herself to display any real emotion other than cheeriness; otherwise, she would face judgment, recrimination and, ultimately, loneliness.

No matter who you are you should never have to apologize for it, and that's what Cynthia found out. She was withholding her greatness – the very best of her – just to be liked. She was apologizing for who she was.

Back to the young women in the airport: Why do I feel sorry for the tall, pretty one? Because the confidence she exudes may have a lot to do with how people react to her. If she's been exalted her whole life simply because of her beauty, it's possible she may never have had the chance or desire to truly find her real gift. And when or if her looks fade, where are her opportunities?

The other girl in the airport, the less attractive one, certainly has other challenges. But she is more likely to look inward and find out who she really is and where her true talents lie. The great masters of Zen will tell you that early success can and often will lead to harder times ahead.

The above are exaggerated examples of a poignant message: "Who are you being just to be liked?"

There's more to go, and we're not quite finished, but by now you should be seeing a little light at the end of the tunnel.

CHAPTER SIX HOMEWORK

Practice saying "Yes" to things that scare you. Do this as many times as you can.

Each day for the next week keep a journal of how many times you hear "No" in your life. Write down how many times you hear "Yes."

Also write down how many times you are a "No" to yourself, and how many times you're a "Yes" to yourself.

Pick a situation this week where someone tells you "No," and see how far you can go in actually getting a "Yes" from them instead. Do it without anger or recrimination, just use your natural charm and your belief in yourself and your goal. Write down how it felt to see it through.

_____

_____

_____

_____

_____

_____

PART THREE: POSITION

For the first two sections of this book we have been getting you closer to understanding who you are and what you want, and allowing you to give yourself the permission to go for what you are destined to achieve. Now comes the part where you position yourself to make it happen. Whether you join a group, network, meet new people, get a new job, or move to a new town, how you position yourself with the knowledge of who you are and the allowance you give yourself to get it is now ultimately the key to your success.

So you're between jobs; you've updated your résumé, gotten a new suit, compiled letters of reference, taken classes, and honed your interview skills. But if you wait for someone to come to you to offer you a job, you're going to be waiting a long time. Or perhaps you've been out of a relationship for a long time; you've been working out, reading all the relationship books, and working on your tan. But if you're still going to same bars, dating sites, or singles groups that you have in the past, you're going to be meeting the same people over and over and asking yourself, "Why haven't I met any decent people?"

Sometimes all it takes if a little turn of the head, and you'll see things in a much different way. Sometimes that turn of the head might need to be toward the mirror. One of the best motivational quotes I've ever heard is, "if you want something you've never had, you have to do something you've never done."

In these last two chapters we're going to be looking at people who chose to step boldly out of their comfort zones, risk everything and create extraordinary outcomes not just for themselves, but in the lives of others as well.

CHAPTER SEVEN

IT'S EASIER TO ASK FOR FORGIVENESS THAN PERMISSION

Throughout the evolution of our species, the adrenal glands emerged as a tool for defense. When a threat was apparent (like an animal attack or fight), a signal was sent from the brain to the adrenal glands to release adrenaline – a self-made dose of Red Bull for the body – into our bloodstream. What this does for the body is "jolt" it into a ready state where muscles are taught and senses are sharp. The process takes but a millisecond, and in that short time the brain can decide to fight or flee – but it's ready for either option.

These days, the adrenals are almost obsolete in terms of what they were originally meant to do. Certainly they are needed as humans still have the need for adrenaline in precarious situations, but the situations most of us face on a day-to-day basis involve a stress produced not from outside influences, but from our own fears, anxieties, and anger! Stress is such a big part of our lives now, but it's not "fight or flight" stress; it's work or home stress. Nonetheless, often times during a stressful situation – like a meeting with your boss, an audition, or public speaking – the adrenaline is released, but there's neither the option of fight NOR flight. But without with option for release, the tension simply mounts within your body and takes a new form.

Fight or flight is much less evident in today's American society. Today do or don't is the question which plagues our brain. The will to act in times of confusion – should I or shouldn't I? – can be as confusing as anything. The knowledge of a bad outcome, the fear of making a mistake, and the unwillingness to face recrimination can halt a person in their tracks. And sometimes that form of paralysis can mean death.

Mel Chang is not the only person I know of who died from stress. I'm sure you know someone, or know someone who knew someone who died from stress-related illness... the condition brought about while knowing that what you're doing is damaging to mind and body, but the phrase "What are you gonna do?" seems to be enough as long as you can still say it. My goal for this particular section of the book is to help understand that at any given moment, you will feel that stress – you know the feeling – and in that moment, you can use your knowledge of what is going on with you physiologically to help adjust yourself psychologically. In other words, being a person of action despite your fears, in the face of extreme opposition, with a clear knowledge of who you are and what your goals are, and the permission to carry them out can not only utilize that stress for the positive, but perhaps relieve it. Because stress can be a killer.

In the world of NLP, we're taught that all energy is either coming to you, or flowing out of you, and if you hang on to any of it, it will manifest in your body and in your life. A great example of this comes from my own experience while taking my NLP certification course.

On the second day of the training, a classmate of mine came in late saying that she had just gotten a speeding ticket. The teacher, Matt James, turned to all of us and warned, "Be careful, class... that energy is now headed your way!" Another classmate raised his hand and asked what he meant by that. This is what he told us:

"All the thought energy created by man in the universe flows to us or away from us. You can't stop it from doing either; you can only be aware of it and adjust accordingly. If you see a couple arguing in a restaurant a few tables away, then the next time you're out you see another couple arguing just a few feet from you, that means the energy is headed your way. If you've just had a fight with your significant other and the next week your best friends have a fight, then the energy is flowing away from you. So if you see a certain energy heading to you, the best thing to do is be aware of it and exude the opposite... be good to the person in your life, and you will avoid or deflect that energy."

I wasn't sure if I really bought that philosophy, and even though I didn't debate it with him, I chalked his little lesson up to "eat the meat, spit out the bones," and I focused on what worked for me.   That night heading home from class, I got a speeding ticket. My first one in eight years!

The next day I told Matt and the class about the experience, and I confessed to him that I thought his story the day before was full of crap. He just smiled.

So if energy is flowing everywhere, positive and negative, then there must be as much good vibes and bad ones. Many of us choose to focus on the negative, and the amount of energy we give our fears can stop us cold in our tracks. It can become as real as we make it; it can keep us from acting in our own best interests; it can be very harmful if we're not careful. And it's because we make our fears real that we get stopped in life. How many times have you heard someone say, "I'd do that, but it scares the heck out of me!" How many times have you said that yourself? And it's because of that fear that somebody else will take advantage of you and your fear. It might be a bully threatening your lunch money out of you; it could be an insurance agent getting you to sign for more coverage than you need; it could be your government frightening you into giving up your civil liberties under the guise of "keeping you safe." Sometimes people will rely on threats to silence you while they knowingly and willingly do harm to others. My next interview is with a man who – in the face of great pressure, and loss of a vast inheritance – fought his own family to warn us all of the dangers of cigarette smoking long before it was popular to do so.

PATRICK REYNOLDS

Patrick Reynolds was born into opulence. As the grandson of tobacco company founder RJ Reynolds, it was expected that he toe the company and family line and work to make the company even greater and more profitable.

But the life of a tobacco industry mogul was the last thing he wanted. Furthermore, Patrick watched his father, RJ Reynolds, Jr., his oldest brother RJ Reynolds III, and other members of his family die from cigarette-induced emphysema and lung cancer. For most of his adult life, he became increasingly aware that the tobacco industry, and RJR specifically, was hiding the evidence of cigarette addiction and in fact finding ways to make them even more addictive. Concerned about the mounting health evidence, he made the decision to speak out against the industry his family helped build. He became the first tobacco industry figure to do so.

In 1952, a secret meeting was held at the Plaza Hotel in New York City, according to Reynolds, in which all involved agreed they would stonewall and disavow any health consequences from smoking. "'It's never been proven that cigarettes cause disease,' they said. 'Of course they were playing with semantics,'" Reynolds claims. "They weren't saying there was no association between smoking and disease, but they were using the word cause semantically in such a way as no one had ever proved that someone put a cigarette in their mouth and got quick sick right away, so they could use the word 'cause' semantically and get away with it," Reynolds adds.

In wasn't until 1964 that the Surgeon's General report brought the dangers to light and, by then, the RJR semantics machine was in full spin mode.

In 1986, Reynolds found himself in Washington D.C. in

the company of Casper Weinberger, then Secretary of Defense, Paul Volker, Chairman of the Federal Reserve, and Republican Senator Robert Packwood, who was working on tax reform. Reynolds was asking questions, and one of the questions he asked was, "If you really are serious about reforming taxes, why don't you raise cigarette taxes?" Packwood responded with his own question to the effect of "you're a Reynolds... why do you care?" Reynolds came to find out that at the time, the tobacco industry was one of the largest donors to the Republican Party – a fact omitted from Packwood's answer. According to Reynolds' research, 75-80 percent of their funds go to Republican candidates in tax whereas Democrats only get 20-25 percent; it influences the way they vote as politicians taking money from big tobacco are five times more likely to vote the way big tobacco wants them to.

Reynolds was actually asked by Packwood to come down that day and speak to Congress about the cigarette tax. Packwood was hoping Reynolds would add to the spin machine and have influence and cause favor for the tobacco companies. What Reynolds did instead was go back to the west coast and spend the next few weeks searching his soul.

He returned to testify before Congress in 1987, joining the increasing numbers of people he inspired who helped bring about the present ban of smoking on all U.S. domestic flights. In 1989, he founded the Foundation for a Smoke-free America, a nonprofit group dedicated to helping kids quit smoking, or never start, while fighting to eliminate eye-level advertising and displays aimed at kids in convenience stores. It was also at that time that Reynolds published his family biography, *The Gilded Leaf*, which spans three generations of the RJ Reynolds family, earning him recognition from the UN's World Health Organization, and Chicago's Mt. Sinai Hospital which awarded him its Humanitarian of the Year award.

He then went on to campaign for numerous state cigarette

tax increases, vending machine bans, 100% smoking bans, and laws to limit youth access and campaign finance reform. He also approached several members of Congress about the aggressive advertising of American brands in the Third World and Asia, and has repeatedly called for state legislators to more adequately fund tobacco education and prevention programs, which have proven to be very effective in reducing youth smoking rates. He organized and moderated a discussion panel and Q&A for the 2002 Conference on Tobacco or Health in San Francisco. Titled "Finding Our Voices: The Need to be More Outspoken," the panel included six leading tobacco-free advocates. Ever vigilant, Reynolds campaigned for Florida's Amendment 6, the historic ballot measure which provided for a statewide 100% smoking ban in Florida restaurants. It was historic because it was the first state to achieve a smoking ban in restaurants through a ballot measure. He also campaigned in four Michigan cities, championing Proposal 4 as a private citizen.

He lobbied Delaware's governor to sign a bill strongly limiting smoking statewide in Delaware, and he debated on CNN's *Talkback Live* in favor of a New York City condo board's right to turn down future condo sales to smokers due to complaints from existing occupants about secondhand smoke passing into their apartments through the building's ventilation system, and he is responsible for the ban on smoking in restaurants and bars in New York City.

In 2001 Reynolds wrote an editorial criticizing President Bush's budget, which de-funded the Justice Department's lawsuit against the tobacco industry. Reynolds wrote, "This move is a brazen protection by the President of Big Tobacco. It means a possible $100 billion savings to them. According to Common Cause, the tobacco companies gave over $5.37 million in campaign donations in 1999 and 2000—with $4.7 million, or 88%, going to Republicans. Is it really just a coincidence that Bush drastically cut the funding of the federal lawsuit against Big

Tobacco? No corporation gives away millions of dollars without a good reason. Department of Justice lawyers say they need $57 million to continue, but Bush is offering just $1.8 million. In truth, it means the end of the federal lawsuit." Later, in July of that year when the Senate Appropriations Committee approved a measure reinforcing Bush's intention, Reynolds issued a press release to call public attention to it.

In late 2003, former Surgeon General C. Everett Koop commented, "Patrick Reynolds is one of the nation's most influential advocates of a smoke-free America. His testimony is invaluable to our society."

Over the years, Reynolds has presented his live talk to over 150,000 college, middle school, and high school students and transformed the way our culture sees and deals with smoking. And he sacrificed virtually everything – including familial relationships and his share of a very large fortune – to do it.

I met Patrick at his Los Angeles home for an early morning interview over coffee. Despite his impressive reputation of anti-smoking vigilance, there was no sign on it on any walls. There were no anti-smoking campaign posters leaning against files of lawsuits and legislation records. Nowhere could I find evidence of the maverick insider who turned his back on an easy and privileged free ride and turned the tobacco company his grandfather created on its ear. Instead, he chooses to surround himself with modest but tasteful antiques, charming and ancient photographs of people who are not his family, and a very unassuming, but confusing coffee press which baffled both of us to the point of distraction until his wife Alexandra was able to step in and show us how it worked.

I sat with him in the sun-lit front room of his single story, modest but charming home in Playa del Rey drinking coffee from the press, wondering aloud how we had so much trouble figuring it out, with one single, unshakable question in my head: "How does someone take on not only one of the largest and most powerful companies in the world, but also his own family?"

I'm eager to talk with you about what many consider to be a heroic act, essentially turning against your family's generations-old business to warn people of the dangers of tobacco and smoking.

First of all, I don't see myself as a hero. I just enjoy the results. When they did surveys of the people who were the whistleblowers on big tobacco and they estimated the public's feelings regarding them, about a third of the people thought that they were wonderful people, about a third of the people thought they just betrayed their loyalties, and about a third didn't really have an opinion. So, I got to make a difference in short and found myself in a position to have a voice that would be heard loud and clear across the nation, but I didn't realize quite how loud and quite how widely that my comments would be broadcast.

What would you say was the turning point for you in your life where you said it was time to speak the truth?

I got in therapy, and the result of getting in therapy was that I began getting in touch with some anger toward my father for not being around.

Your dad was gone from the time you were age three until age six?

Yeah, and I was learning to set boundaries in therapy. I found my voice and went back to LA after turning Robert Packwood down, and I began looking into the tobacco industry. The more I learned, the angrier I became. I was getting in touch with my feelings about my father and getting clarity about a lot

STOP WAITING FOR PERMISSION!

of things. Part of that clarity at the time was for me to see the reality of the tobacco industry. And when Packwood invited me to speak publicly in Washington, even though I turned him down, it was a defining moment because I realized that I could make a difference and, if I wanted to, I could speak out publicly and probably make a strong difference at a time when nobody was speaking out against the tobacco industry-no members of it were anyway.

In the Reynolds family, what was the family mindset? Was it just unspoken? You don't talk about the dangers of tobacco?

Remember that my father had been married four times, so we weren't a close family.   My real family was my brother and my mother. They were my core family. If you're from a rich family, if you're among the wealthy, very often, if you also have money, it almost doesn't matter how you made it, you could have been in the mafia.   But they will love you and honor you and accept you into their fold because you have money. My mother came from a very poor family in New York. She fought her way up as an actress to Warner Bros., had some success on the Broadway stage and then Hollywood.   So, she wasn't one of the Reynolds family and they didn't like her. And in 1970 there was a family reunion in North Carolina organized by my aunt, one of the ten most generous living Americans at the time and giving money away like it was water. I had been in Berkeley for a couple of years as a college student. I was growing my hair long and smoking pot and catching the spirit of free love as well as my studies and rowing on the crew team, becoming an athlete, so it was all these things going on.... and smoking. That's when I started smoking cigarettes. And even though I wore a suit, they looked at me like I was from Jupiter. I was following my own drummer.

Were you the only one in the family doing that?

Yeah, later I went to see my brothers and talk to each of them.

What did they say when you told them you were going to blow the whistle?

Oh, we had some heated discussions.

Why, was at stake for them?

They still held stock in the company. They were concerned the stock price was, you know, going to fall.

Did they try to talk you out of it?

Oh yeah, I mean they said, 'you're going to be an embarrassment to the family.' They didn't want anything to do with it. They were only worried about the money, but the price of the stock didn't go down. It kept skyrocketing, so they all made millions.

Despite you?

I had nothing to do with it.

Were you considered an embarrassment to the family then?

No. I received many awards, honors, accolades. I got an award from the World Health Organization and many others. I mean, I've got a drawer full of plaques around here. And then, as far as the price of the stock, the stock kept going up, so I think that they kind of relaxed a little bit as time went by, and we joshed around about it a little bit, but they never publicly endorsed me. My brother Mike was publicly supportive.

What were you seeking when you went to your brothers?

I just wanted to let them know that this is something I was going to be doing. And....they didn't like it and they were threatened by it and worried by it, because I would be rocking the boat pretty heavily.

Even though they said don't do this.

Yes, and I mean it was also doing battle with the spirit of my father and the spirit of my grandfather. And I've been asked in news reports and shows that say, 'Don't you think your grandfather is up in heaven rolling in his grave and freaking out?' And, you know, what I say is no. He's not concerned with making a profit anymore, and I think he's my greatest champion, saying 'I didn't know cigarettes were going to kill hundreds of millions of people, you go for it grandson. You continue campaigning for higher state cigarette taxes around the nation, championing ballot measures and legislative assembly bills to bring about smoking bans statewide, banning smoking in all bars and restaurants. You go for it. You know, because this is the right thing to do.'

I love the quote 'Virtue is its own reward.' And I never got that or understood what that meant and finally it came to me. My former therapist said to me when you lie or when you cheat or when you steal, you have to carry that around with you. And I teach that to high school kids now – it's part of my talk. You don't feel good about yourself, you know, if you're carrying around some deep, dark secret that you never told anybody, that's like carrying around a 500 pound weight. Set the weight down and talk to another person. It will set you free. It will feel so good.

Where did you learn this?

From my therapist and from also experience.

But you had this in you.

True.

Your brother said No to you, don't do this.... and you said I'm going to do it anyway. What gave you that strength to go against your family and risk losing money, them, everything?

Because, I think that, you know, all of us out there... over here you're a child and over there you're an adult and you're crossing that bridge, and I walk across the stage and I say you're crossing that bridge towards being adults. And as you cross the bridge you're going to look back and say 'No, Mom, you want me home at 8 o'clock. I'm not going to be home till 10 o'clock. I'm sorry," and you walk a little further across and you say, 'Maybe I'm not coming home at all.' And finally over here you're an adult and you're making all your own decisions, so it really is as you change over from being a child to being a full-fledged adult you are going to necessarily speak out and say, tell your truth and set your boundaries with other people and learn to say No.

Were you scared after your brother said not to do the Good Morning America *Interview in 1986?*

You know, I broke out in hives on the plane to New York. It was terrifying. I had been prepared by the American Lung Association's media trainer and, fortunately, I had been groomed, because they know, sophisticated people in media and in politics know, they can predict quite easily what questions you're going to be asked. For example, 'Well, Mr. Reynolds, you're in this for publicity. You're not really sincere. Come on this whole thing is very disingenuous.' I froze and I was like, what am I going to say to that? I felt guilty. I felt so guilty and wrong. They made me feel wrong by asking me this question when I knew I was right. And the answer that I came up with was, 'My only memories of my father were the man laying down dying from smoking. I care about this issue. Don't you dare challenge me.' And I projected authenticity and it went over beautifully and they never asked me that again.

It seems to me that we're losing the ability to question our leaders. We're losing the ability to think for ourselves. We're losing the ability to stand up and work from our instincts and go with our gut. How do you see the culture now in terms of our ability to stand up, to do what's right, fight for what's right, be aware of what's right? Is it in disrepair, is it messed up, are we healthy, are we okay?

Florida was one of the states that had been spending the most money on tobacco prevention. They were having fantastic success. But at first the health community in Florida, and this is what we're getting at here, remained mute, hardly anybody would speak out about this. They were not speaking up, not organizing. Well, why did they stay quiet and why did they stay so silent? People are afraid of losing their jobs, so created a seminar called 'How You can be More Politically Outspoken without Losing your Job,' and I got a bunch of advocates together and we held a national panel. But the point was I said you can speak out in your own private time, when you're not under government payroll time, as a private citizen at night you're free to say whatever you want to say if you only make the effort to do it. So, I think there is a lot of apathy politically out there and there's a long, long tradition of apathy.

But why do we buy into the apathy?

I think it goes beyond just apathy. I think we're living in a time when people are more and more overwhelmed. Ironically, computers have given us such a wide reach, and yet they somehow are sucking up more of our time. It seems to me in the old days we may have got a lot less done, but there was more free time. There was more time for family and now people are working till 7 o'clock at night or later. People are putting in a lot more hours and I think it's because the computers have enabled people to do two people's jobs. There are a lot of factors. I haven't got the answers, but it's also the sheer weight of all those things that press down on us that competes for our time in this age that we live in. It's a hard time, so standing up to the No's in life and keeping your boundaries is harder than ever. I endorse and champion what you're doing with this book because hopefully it will inspire thousands of people to find their voice and to find their bliss.

• • •

It's been said many times that courage is not the opposite of fear; instead courage is *acting in the face of fear.* The same energy that drives your anxiety can fuel your empowerment. The energy doesn't have consciousness; it goes where you direct it. The key is in how you manage what you've got. Patrick Reynolds nearly lost his lunch on the plane heading to New York where he was going to blow the whistle on his family's business, but he knew in his heart that what he was doing was the right thing; his actions – while estranging him from family and fortune – would save lives.

On June 13, 2009, right around the time the orinigal draft of this book was going to press, and after eleven years of relentless dedication to his anti-smoking efforts, Reynolds was thrilled at this announcement by the FDA:

The House and Senate agreed on Friday on a final version of the bill and sent it on to President Obama, who is expected to sign it into law shortly. The bill gives the FDA new powers to regulate ingredients in tobacco products, and reduce, but not eliminate, nicotine. It will also eliminate candy flavorings and ban labeling such as "low tar" and "light," which lead many smokers to believe those brands are safer. The bill also requires cigarette packs to carry graphic warning labels on 50% of both the front and back faces of all cigarette packages, and calls for strict new limits on full-color tobacco advertising. Many print tobacco ads will now be in black and white.

Reynolds has also brought about anti-smoking reform in Russia, India, China, and the Middle East. I called him just after I had read the news. Not surprisingly, he was over the moon about the huge step his efforts helped to create.

The most impressive thing about Reynolds' accomplishments has always been his singular focus, his direction.

So how do we steer *ourselves* in the right direction? That's what the final chapter is all about.

CHAPTER SEVEN HOMEWORK

List five things you want that you would fight for.

1. _____

2. _____

3. _____

4. _____

5. _____

Now list one thing that you want that you would die for. Why? What does this one thing mean to you?

_____

_____

_____

_____

Go back over your previous worksheets, notes, and homework. Begin to see old patterns, ways of thinking and actions that defined you as a person who was willing to take no for an answer in life. Also notice that you're beginning to think of things you will do differently. You see... you did this all on your own, no one gave this to you. You're creating it.

CHAPTER EIGHT

INSTINCTS: TO TRUST OR NOT TO TRUST?

BEING IN THE GAME

I'm a New England Patriots fan – have been since the year they first went to the Superbowl against the Chicago Bears in 1986. My very first game was their opening game of that season. My buddy Chris Braga – a Pats fan since birth – invited me to the game because he knew I had a car. It was the very first football game I ever saw in person. The Patriots beat their fierce divisional rivals, the New York Jets, and I turned to Chris at the end of the game and said "Wouldn't it be great if they went to the Suberbowl this year?" He laughed and pointed out that the Pats had never been to the big game, and this season would be no different. Chris had long suffered through 2-14 seasons, losing all hope that his team would one day be great.

But the Patriots *did* end up going to the Superbowl for the first time that year, and I have been a tried and true fan ever since, dreaming that perhaps my attendance on the first game of that special season played a small part in their success.

Years later I became friends with a very powerful motivational speaker and business coach (and former New England Patriot!) by the name of Jeff Hoffman. Jeff now lives in Brentwood, California and is a successful entrepreneur and speaker. At one of his seminars, I heard him tell a fantastic but true story of a friend of his, a football player by the name of Paul Hofer.

In 1982, Hofer had a chance to try out for the position of running back on the San Francisco 49ers. It was a tough training camp, and Hofer did his best to earn a spot on the team. He had stiff competition, however, from another RB who already had the spot the year before. Paul Hofer showed up every day, sometimes twice a day, and worked his hardest to earn the respect of the other players and coaches. And he got it. Many of the coaches told him that they thought he was the hardest working player on the squad. But it wasn't enough to earn him the spot, and when the final cuts for the season came down, and it was down to Hofer and the other player. The coaches chose the player with the experience over Hofer the rookie.

Paul Hofer found out about his cut the day before the last pre-season match-up. That night he went back to his hotel room and decided not to go sit on the bench the next day. Filled with disappointment, he packed his bags and called a cab to go home.

But something stopped him. He realized that he had played all spring with the other players – some of whom he would call friends – and he didn't want to leave without saying goodbye. He decided that he would end on a strong, high note and suit up for the final pre-season game anyway, even if he was just going to sit on the bench the whole game.

The next day, Hofer showed up, suited up, and as usual sat on the bench during the game. The 49ers were losing, and by the end of the first half, it seem that they were going to go down to defeat and start the season with a negative (even though most people think that pre-season doesn't mean much). At the start of the second half, the 49ers coaches decided that in order to shake things up, they wanted to adjust from an air attack to a running game and began to call for the running back who beat Hofer out for the position. The coaches were yelling and yelling his name, but he wasn't there. Turns out that player was off in a corner talking with a cheerleader. Hofer saw this and knew it was his chance. He ran up to the coaches and without letting them think about it, he simply yelled, "I'm here, coach, I'm going in!"

By the time Hofer got to the huddle, the coaches had called a passing play because they thought they didn't have their running back, but upon seeing Hofer enter the huddle, the quarterback changed the play, and at the snap of the ball, handed the ball off to Hofer. In one amazing run, Hofer not only got the first down, but he managed to elude several tacklers, get free, and get to the end zone.

Touchdown!

After the score, Hofer came back to the sidelines. The head coach grabbed his facemask; Hofer thought for sure he was in trouble. But the coach smiled and said, "Whatever you just did, please do a lot more!" And he did. Hofer played the rest of the game, scored two more touchdowns, and the 49ers won their final pre-season game.

Paul Hofer not only helped the team win the game, but he also earned the spot on the roster as running back. He played six seasons for the San Francisco 49ers, helping them win many games, including Superbowl XVl. As for the other player... no one I've spoken with about this story can remember his name.

Purpose. Permission. Position. You'll never need a better example of how that can work for you than Paul Hofer. He worked his butt off, knew he belonged there, stayed even when he was cut, and made sure he was in the right place at the right time.

What if Hofer had just gone home that night? I still get the chills when I think about that story.

You

We talked about adrenaline earlier, and now I want to tell you what I think adrenaline is still useful for (if you're not using it to fight or flee).

In the moment of decision – that millisecond where various options run by your internal scanner at a dizzying pace – you are aware of all that is possible for you. You know what you are capable of, and what you're not. Your adrenaline fuels the brain as well as the muscles, and your decision-making can be as rapid as any computer – faster, really.

Scenarios could range from a good come back to an insult, or the overriding wisdom to say "I need a minute to really think about this," something a lot of us don't give ourselves the permission to do when under the gun.

Your instincts show up as the voice that gives you the first answer. That's right. The first answer. Ever watch *Jeopardy?* Alex Trebec throws out the question, and the first thing that comes to your mind is immediately overruled by a logical dismantling of the answer. Your mind thinks, "That can't be it, it's too easy," or "Wait, that's stupid, it's probably this," or "I'm usually wrong, so I'll guess this instead," but it turns out that the answer you first had was the right one. That's your instinct working for you.

Instincts tell us if we should be with the person we're with, if we should buy that house, take that job, tell the truth, fight for a cause, stay out of a fight, write a book, go for the gold, say goodbye to a friendship that no longer serves us, and so many others. The best test for knowing your own instinctual guide is to know yourself.

There has been, however, some opposition to the notion

that trusting your instincts is the right thing to do. An author by the name of Steve Friedman, in his book *The Agony of Victory* (Arcade), claims that trusting his instincts led to disaster for him. Here is an excerpt:

There is a how-to philosophy that has recently enjoyed a kind of grassroots traction in this country. It is as sensible-sounding as it is potentially disastrous. I'm speaking of the advice to Trust Your Instincts. This folksy nostrum gained pop-literary luster two years ago, with the publication of Malcolm Gladwell's Blink: The Power of Thinking without Thinking *(Little, Brown and Company), a work dedicated to the idea that our first impulses often represent approximately a gazillion infinitesimal and subconscious calculations, and consequently should be treated with a great deal of respect. In July, a German social psychologist named Gerd Gigerenzer took up the issue. In* Gut Feelings: The Intelligence of the Unconscious *(Viking Adult), he argues that while a rational approach to decision-making might sound... well, rational... the best decisions come from our first impulses.*

That sounds good. For certain types of people, however, it is very bad. Consider some unsettling decisions that have recently plagued a decent, well-intentioned and fairly typical middle-aged man I know well and for whom I often feel an odd combination of irritation, pity, and all-encompassing love. Let's call him "Steve."

For example, should Steve brew himself a soothing cup of herbal tea and go to bed early tonight? Or should he follow his instincts and order a pint of Chunky Monkey from the deli across the street and settle in for a few drowsy hours staring slack jawed at season four of The Simpsons? His instincts suggest the latter.

And what about tomorrow? Should Steve shave and

shower and put on a freshly laundered button-down shirt and prepare to meet the niece of a good friend of his ever-helpful mother – a "nice girl, sweet, ready to settle down"? Or should Steve punch his keyboard and go online looking for cheap thrills, only to find himself in the predawn darkness exchanging bon mots with "host tamale from the bronx23" who likes "fast cars, bad boys, and fine wines?" Steve faces vexing choices like these more often than he would like to admit. I think it's fair to say that Steve wrestles with them on a daily basis.

My instincts, it is safe to say, failed me for many, many years. I knew this. I had followed my baser impulses too slavishly. I had listened to friends who suggested, when I was in crisis mode (which was often) that I "listen to my gut." I had been, contrary to my beloved father's chronic and worried and gently advice, more fiddle-playing grasshopper than nut-hoarding ant. I needed to fight my instincts. I needed to grow up.

I trusted my instincts for two years, and now I am fat and near homeless. It might be a good idea to distrust my instincts for a while.

. . .

Which of those two voices represents his instincts talking? The FIRST of course! He lists them! To sit there smugly and rattle off secondary options that he'd rather do doesn't represent his true instincts; they represent his lack of will to pursue and achieve his greatest good. The fact that he lists the powerful positive choices *first* tells you that those are his instinctual notions of what he should be doing! He lists the lazy, sedentary reasons second. Always!

For whatever reason, and I'm hoping it's for a tongue-in-cheek manifesto for the lazily dispossessed, Friedman is perpetuating the notion that those of us out there who are dedicated to helping others achieve their greatest good are somehow just throwing a bunch of crap at the wall, hoping something will stick. Unfortunately, it seems Mr. Friedman completely missed the point, and at the same time found a way to hang blame on someone else for his own vices. Let this be a cautionary tale for you working so hard to improve.

A FINAL PUSH

You know I finally did get a chance to try to interview Arnold Schwarzenegger.

Remember, this was before the scandal that broke up his marriage. It's funny, I kinda feel like I have to keep saying that. Oh well... you get it.

It took three years, several missed last-second opportunities, countless unreturned calls to his press office, and just as many conversations with his assistants, PR staff and handlers who all gave the same response verbatim: "The Governor thanks you for your interest, but unfortunately due to his busy schedule, he won't be able to give an interview at this time." Fair enough.

But I never lost hope. As I continued writing the book, I would enlist the help of friends in the news corps who might be able to bring me along – press pass in hand – to a press conference. No joy there. I tried to take the easy way out by using public quotes of his from other interviews, but either the questions weren't appropriate for the book's purposes, or I just didn't like the thought of not actually getting the interview. I think the latter is the real answer.

So finally in November of 2008 I once again attended the California Governor and First Lady's Conference on Women. As I mentioned earlier,, 2008 was the year that the Governor was going to be at the conference (no wild fires to attend to, luckily), so I was determined to get the interview.

All day I kept a watchful eye, hoping that at any moment Mr. Schwarzenegger would appear, and I could run up and ask my questions quickly. I even interviewed Maria first. When I mentioned to her that I had planned to get the Governor to answer some questions, she cryptically replied with a roll of her eyes, "Good luck."

The time had come. Arnold had entered the building and was quickly whisked to the convention center floor where he would tour the latest innovations in green technology and other advances where California was leading the way, and women were endorsing them. A quiet, unassuming volunteer named Diana decided that my pursuit of the Governor was too exciting to miss, so she decided to tag along for fun, not really knowing why I was so eager to interview him.

Seeing the Governor, much less getting to him, was difficult. He was surrounded by a throng of secret service guards, assistants, and his Deputy Press Secretary who, upon seeing me walk up with my microphone and portable recorder, said very politely: "The Governor thanks you for your interest, but unfortunately due to his busy schedule, he won't be able to give an interview at this time." Seriously, she said that.

"Got it," I responded immediately. "I just have two questions, that's it." She dismissed me with a frown and continued along with the group surrounding the Governor. They moved like a group of birds, all linked perhaps telepathically, moving from foot to foot in lock step with Arnold. If he stopped, they stopped. If he moved, they moved. If he turned his head, they looked that way too. If he pivoted, they adjusted. It was a silent dance that tickled my observational funny bone. "He's not giving any interviews today," the DPS now communicated in a much more frustrated tone.

"Right, no problem... if you don't mind, I'm going to just follow."

And this continued for nearly twenty minutes. Everywhere Arnold went, his entourage – plus one – followed. At several points during the "stalking," a couple of the security men looked over their shoulder at me as if to say "I'm allowing you to live right now because you're keeping your distance, but any closer and you'll lose something you need."

But before I knew it, I was one of them! On and on we went, and I was occasionally glad to see that Diana had also chosen to continue as well, staying put on my left flank the whole time, perhaps just as anxious to see Mr. Schwarzenegger as I was.

But then something happened. The Governor decided that his tour of the convention floor was over and he abruptly turned to the exit, shifting the entire group like a "Roomba" that just hit the wall and doubled back. I panicked – internally of course –I didn't know what to do. I could see clearly that my persistence might not pay off, and this might be my last chance at interviewing Arnold Schwarzenegger, the man whose very life embodies what my entire book is about. For nearly three years I wrote and wrote and rewrote and edited and wrote again this book with the absolute unshakable goal of putting the Governor's quote from my interview in as an inspiration. I knew it would happen; I counted on it perhaps more than I ever realized, and now it seemed like it was vanishing.

I looked at the Deputy Press Secretary, who was now tapping away on her Blackberry, no doubt signaling the limo to be ready. She signaled "No" to me and moved on.

That second lasted about a week in my mind. My heart rate increased dramatically; I felt flushed and clammy. My breath was short and my mind was racing. It wasn't surprising to me that I felt so strongly about it, but I hadn't expected to be so disappointed. And in that moment, for one infinitesimal second I said to myself "You didn't make it... it's over. Give up, you're not going to get it." I could feel my shoulders slump and my head lower a bit. Of all the thoughts racing through my head, the loudest was: "You've let your readers down." You. I let you down. All the research, the work with clients like Melissa, Nate, and Carol, the hustling to get interviews with Gail Zappa, Burt Rutan, Maria Shriver, Jenny McCarthy and the rest. There were the endless plane flights where, for hours at a time, I would write and rewrite this book to get my point just right... the sleepless nights where, fueled by dedication and inspiration, I scribbled notes to myself in the light of a street lamp outside my hotel window. And there was the undeniable issue of pride... not quitting, as it turns out, says as much about my ego as it does my drive to succeed. I knew I would finish the book, but without achieving one of the earliest and strongest goals for the book, I began to wonder, "What's the point?"

And there I lived in that empty moment, in the timeless vacuum of self-doubt and failure, until I felt a tap on my shoulder. I turned around to see Diana still standing there next to me. "Don't give up..." she said quietly. "Do it." I looked at her puzzled, as if she really knew who I was, what I was doing this for and why, but she couldn't have known. What she did know was that I wanted this... she could see it. And she could see my disappointment. And in that moment, a woman who volunteered to help me out with whatever I wanted gave me exactly what I needed: A final push.

I took a deep breath, spun around and caught up with the DPS. She saw me coming and sighed as if defeated and said, "Okay... two questions. Move up to match the secret service, when he gets to the exit door, step two steps in front of him and ask only two questions. Go NOW!"

I was off like a shot, leaving Diana, the DPS and my defeat behind me. I did as I was instructed, matched pace with the lead security guard and at the right moment, moved into position for my interview. Suddenly I was aware of the same sweaty palms and erratic heartbeat, but it was now the pulse of eminent victory. I was literally a foot away from my ultimate goal!

That's when they pulled me outside and beat the hell out of me.

Just kidding.

No, to my surprise, I was warmly met by the Governor who continued to walk as I lobbed my first question:

Governor, your life is an amazing example of not taking No for an answer. Can you tell me how you developed that philosophy?

I think you learn everything in sports. If you want to succeed in sports, the only way to succeed is that if you fail, and you fail, and you fail, you get up every time and you just keep moving on and eventually you will see victory. And the same is also true in real life. You've got to just always move on, be positive, and see a finished product in front of you and just go after it - that's the key thing.

The Governor's answer surprised me. I always thought he would attribute his stalwartness to his mother or father, or his relationship to the Kennedy clan. But of course, sports! When he gave me his answer, it all made perfect sense. I remembered Paul Hofer and his amazing tale of persistence. I began to imagine in my head the 60-minute clock in football, which ticks relentlessly until the end of the game. And all the players on the teams know that win or lose they have to play the entire 60 minutes, and nothing less. And within that 60-minute time period they come to know – week after week, year after year – what they're made of and how far they can push themselves, even when their head, their hearts, and their muscles might be telling them otherwise. The real athletes don't come to win, they come to compete!

I had a follow up:

Has there been a time in your life ever that you didn't think you were going to get up?

No, I always knew I was going to get up. It was just always a question of how. You have setbacks sometimes and sometimes you are down, but I was always fortunate to have more victories than defeats.

• • •

After the last answer, he was whisked off to his car and driven away. But I got it. I got the interview!

The statement that struck me the most was "It was always a question of how." How. *It's not if you can do something, it's how!* At the point when Aron Ralston decided to live, and he needed to take action, the question wasn't if he should do it, but how he was going to free himself. Kathy Buckley never asked, "Why is this happening to me," but instead "How can I make this disability actually work for me?" Burt Rutan always knew he was going to build a spacecraft, the question wasn't "Should I be doing this," it was always "How can I do this?" Jenny McCarthy never stopped for a moment to feel sorry for herself, nor did she simply take "No" for an answer despite her own maternal instincts; she asked herself and others "How can I overcome this obstacle and help my son emerge from the fog of autism?" And then there was Paul Hofer; by making sure he was in the right place at the right time, he was simply asking "How can I make the best of the situation I'm in?" As a result, he put his pride aside, supported his teammates, and ultimately got what he wanted despite the first, second, fifth and twentieth "No."

And every other brave man and woman I have had the honor to speak with and work with while writing this book eventually let go of the denial and the fear and boldly asked the question; "How can I get this done?"

THE ART OF THE POSSIBLE

John F. Kennedy once compared the impossible task of getting to the moon to walking down a dead-end alley: "If you're walking down an alley and you reach a wall that's too high to get over," he said, "and there's no other way around, throw your hat over the wall, then you'll find a way over."

"How?" is the key question we all should be asking every time we're challenged. Instead of "Why is this happening to me," try asking "How can I make this work in my favor?" Instead of waiting for the permission from other people or circumstances to comfortably step into your desired situation, challenge yourself and others with "How are we going to make this happen?" Most often the best answer is "I don't know," because you've left no option for "No." Instead, you've steered the conversation into the realm of what is possible.

Arnold Schwarzenegger never once even entertained the possibility of accepting "No" as an answer. For him, it was always just a question of *how* he was going to get things done, not *if*.

Even while writing this book I asked myself many times "How can I best inspire my readers to empower themselves?" I never once asked if I should – or even if I *could* – write this book, I just decided that I was going to.

So how can you get the most out of this book? You can start by taking "Yes" for an answer from yourself as well as from others. After all, being challenged in life is inevitable. Being defeated is optional.

For the twenty-five years I have been involved in personal growth, I have tried every day to be a better person. Not because I think the one I am now is not so great, but because I know I'm not done yet. The one thing I know for sure is that I don't really know anything. The more I learn, the more I realize that there's so much more to learn. Socrates said, "The unexamined life is not worth living." Life is here for us to discover.

I don't know about you, but I am so sick of people thriving on negativity and settling for mediocrity simply because anything more is threatening. I'm disappointed with the lack of ethics and true journalism in what we call news today. I'm saddened by the unrest and atrocities still committed by man on his fellow man all over this planet. I'm disappointed in our machine mentality in politics.

I'm confused by the apathy in most people to not stand up and fight for what they believe in. I'm baffled by parents who fear disciplining their children because they need to be liked by them. And I'm fed up with the attitude, "Hey, I'm only human, what more do you want from me?" The point of being human – the only species we know of with self-awareness and the astounding ability to achieve what he have to this point – is to grow, to learn, to be better than we feel like being. And not necessarily just because we can, but because we *should*. Our cognitive understanding of how rare and precious our time on this rock in space in the middle of absolutely nowhere is a gift! Once you know there's a better choice for you and you choose not to take it, you're selling out on your greatness, and worse, you're losing the opportunity to inspire greatness in others who follow. As Emily Dickinson wrote: "I dwell in possibility."

In this race of life, you've never been a bad runner; maybe you just trained for the wrong race. Forget the old race... pick a new finish line and train for that. Ask yourself after reading this book and doing all the homework "Who am I really? What do I really want, and if I don't have it, what will it take to get it? And while I'm at it, what little thing can I do each day to connect more with those around me, and live in each moment as if it were the only moment in my life?"

The answer is in your instincts. It's in your heart and in your dreams. It's in the longing you have for the realization of childhood ambitions and it's in the future you can begin to create *right now*. It's in the love that you feel for life, even if life seems to not always love you back. And don't forget, you might now be living the life you were destined to live, but never appreciated because you were focusing on what you didn't have. If that's the case, being strong enough to choose your life powerfully as it is now is just as courageous as taking on a new one. And in the end, remember... No matter who you powerfully choose to be, know that you're the one holding the starter's gun. When you're ready, pull the trigger. Your life is the race. Your finish line is your legacy.

So go ahead... What are you waiting for?

EPILOGUE

YOUR LEGACY

Perhaps you are familiar with the Serenity Prayer: "God, grant me the serenity to accept the things I cannot change, courage to change the things I can, and the wisdom to know the difference."

Mel Chang and many others like him have left us a legacy to learn from. The reasons you have for not acting on your truest passions and greatest dreams aren't strong enough to erase them. If so, you would be happy right now with who you are and what you have. Totally happy. Instead you're still searching for meaning or a different life that seems better than the one you have.

Your life now is all about knowing the difference, and then having the courage to act on it. Remember, courage is not the opposite of fear; it is the will to act in the face fear. There have been times in your life, as there will be again, where you are called upon to act in the face of fear. But what is the fear, really? Where is it? I think we both know that fear is created solely in our own heads and hearts. So if we can create the fear, then it stands to reason that we can also manage it, and in some instances overcome it, or at least use it to our advantage. Fear can be your fuel. That energy has to go somewhere, why not use it to drive you into the direction of your most powerful and truest destiny? As I said earlier in the book, it's easy to play small, not risking anything, but if you fail without trying, you deserve it. If you fail while taking a risk, then you can learn from it, and that is when anything is possible. And remember also that sometimes the most courageous action you can take in your life is accepting the life you have right now and working to improve the lives of others less fortunate.

Purpose, Permission, Position. However those words touch you, these are the keys to your prosperity, whatever that is for you.

See you at the finish line.

AUTHOR'S NOTE:

The cases mentioned in this work are all based on real people and their experiences. Each client was consulted and gave consent for this book. Each celebrity contribution was done with full consent. Each reference to my own experience in this book is true.

Great thanks to: Steve Rohr and Chris Freeman of Havenhurst Books; Kristi Blicharski of Bliss Media L.A.; Jeremy Coleman, Theresa Carson, and Frank Raphael at Sirius/XM Radio; Paul Stephenson at Harvest Moon Design; my attorney Scott Schwimer, Esq.

And Leeza Gibbons.

And a special thank you to everyone who ever told me "No" in my life.

www.ingramcontent.com/pod-product-compliance
Lightning Source LLC
LaVergne TN
LVHW011228080426
835509LV00005B/383